Daniel Petre has enjoyed a successful ca[...] [...]tion technology and media industries. He spent a number of years in senior positions at Microsoft and PBL (Publishing and Broadcasting Limited), while also participating in various government advisory forums and committees. Daniel currently works as a strategic advisor to company boards and private equity firms. He lives with his wife Carolyn and their three daughters in Sydney.

Also by Daniel Petre

The Clever Country: Australia's digital future
    (with David Harrington)
Father Time
Father and Child

WHAT
MATTERS

SUCCESS AND WORK-LIFE BALANCE

DANIEL PETRE
WITH MIKE HANLEY

Jane Curry Publishing

This book is firstly dedicated to my family: Carolyn,
Grace, Eliza and Alice. Through you I am a better person.
Secondly, it is dedicated to my father-in-law, David, a great success
and role model for all men.

First published by Jane Curry Publishing Pty Ltd 2004
220a Glenmore Road, Paddington, NSW 2021

National Library of Australia
cataloguing-in-publication data:

Petre, Daniel.
What matters: success and work-life balance.

ISBN 1 920727 08 6.

1. Life skills. 2. Quality of life. 3. Quality of work life
I. Title

158.1

'At the Top' from *Poems 1972-2002* by Michael Leunig is reproduced
with permission from Penguin Australia PTY LTD
Cover and internal design by i2i design
Cover image: Getty Images
Typeset in 11/16pt Minion by Midland Typesetters
Printed in Australia by McPherson's Printing Group

THE PETRE FOUNDATION

Over a period of five years, I put all my remuneration from ecorp, and all the shares and options I received, into the Petre Foundation. The foundation acts as a focal point for our family's charitable contributions. Each year the income earned from the foundation is allocated to needy causes. The funds are limited but, proportional to our net worth, the foundation and its annual giving is significant.

Each year we identify some causes with which we feel strongly aligned and look for the most efficient provider of services to that cause. Then we work with the organisation in question to ensure that the funds are directed appropriately.

So far the Petre Foundation has established a Chair in Paediatric Neurology at the Children's Hospital at West-mead, a Chair in Breast Cancer at the Garvan Institute, and a scholarship at the University of New South Wales. We have also donated to a number of youth charities, including Pathways to Manhood and Reach Out, a youth suicide prevention group.

All proceeds from this book will go to the Petre Foundation.

ACKNOWLEDGEMENTS

My great thanks to Jane Curry for her support and motivation over the years, and for creating the opportunity for me to share my views on this complex issue. To Mike Hanley, whose great skill as a writer is matched by his extraordinary patience. If the ideas in this book resonate with readers then great credit must go to Mike for helping form the ideas and bring them to life.

To Elspeth Menzies for her patience and skill in helping pull the project's words and ideas into a final form that is, hopefully, of value to leaders and aspiring leaders around Australia. Finally, my thanks to Jon Gibbs for his wonderful effort in editing the manuscript.

CONTENTS

AT THE TOP

At the top of the tallest building in the world
Sat the saddest man in the world
And inside the man
Was the loneliest heart in the world
And inside the heart
Was the deepest pit in the world

And at the bottom of the pit
Was the blackest mud in the world
And in the mud lay the lightest, loveliest, tenderist,
Most beautiful, happy angel in the universe

Michael Leunig

INTRODUCTION

A very good friend of mine – let's call him Tim – has had an extraordinary career. He has worked for a leading investment bank in Europe for the last ten years and has amassed a considerable fortune along the way. About two years ago Tim and his wife Sara started a family, and at the same time a promotion to run a large part of the bank saw them move to Tokyo. On a recent visit there I caught up with them to see how they were getting on.

Tim is enjoying his job immensely but Sara is finding life very hard away from family and friends now that they have two very young children, and wants to come home. All up, Tim and Sara have been away from Australia for over thirteen years. Over dinner the three of us had a long discussion about where their life was heading and what they wanted, during which it became obvious to me that there was a significant divide in their perspectives. Sara's view is that they have achieved unbelievable financial success and can now come back to Australia and establish a great environment for their children, with friends and family around them. She believes that Tim can leave the bank and spend time developing other interests (he has a deep interest in music, for instance). Tim's view is different. He enjoys the rewards of success and agrees that at some point in time they will head back to Australia – but not yet. In his words. 'I have not yet achieved enough and I want to be more of a success.'

What they will end up doing I am not sure, but I worry that they'll find themselves on a path that I have seen so many executives and their partners travel down. That is, Tim's quest for a 'successful' career could lead to his inability to effectively measure the cost of success or even to define success in terms of a whole-of-life experience; moreover, an inability to work out when he has enough 'stuff'.

My journey was not so different from that of my friend in Tokyo. From my earliest recollections, it seems, I not only wanted to be a success, but I also judged whether others had been more or less successful than their skills and opportunities suggested they should be. I studied the lives of successful people (read: prominent business people), looking for clues to the holy grail – why did some people make it to the big time and others not? My father-in-law, David, was one of those people I judged early on as someone who just didn't make the grade as a success. Nice guy but not a *success*.

David is a very smart and very capable senior executive. From the first time I met him it was obvious that he was very good with people – charming, in fact – and very numerate. Capable, energetic, well connected. And yet, he seemed to be wasting it all. As CEO of a mid-sized subsidiary of a Canadian paper products company, he was doing well, but I knew that someone with his talent could do much better. I felt certain that he could easily pitch himself for a bigger CEO role and make a lot more money, attract more prestige . . . basically, be more successful.

The family lived in a warm, inviting bungalow with a pool, on the north shore of Sydney, spacious and suburban but nothing over the top. He drove a safe middle-range European car – again, nothing over the top. The family was well off, certainly, but there were plenty of people with a lot more and I couldn't understand why David didn't want more than to just do okay. Here was a man who had the skills and drive of a senior business executive, but it seemed to me that he never put it into top gear; instead he chose to cruise.

Over the years, as my relationship with his daughter Carolyn developed (we got married and have three gorgeous girls), I got to know David a lot better. Now, 23 years later, I no longer see him as someone who could have had more success. In fact, he's one of the most successful executives I have ever met. Don't get me wrong, I am not championing mediocrity. Just the opposite. I am a great believer in always doing your absolute best and always pushing yourself outside your comfort zone in order to develop new and greater skills. However, I also believe that focusing on one aspect of your life – work in particular – at the expense of everything else *does not* bring about a successful life. Such focus *may* bring success in one aspect of your life but not your whole life.

As a way of explaining this turnaround in my definition of success, let's compare David with another top executive, Wayne. I met Wayne at a big corporate shindig at Sydney's Regent Hotel in 1994. The CEO of a large Australian company, he was the wealthy and powerful executive that David could have been. (To be fair, David is a lot smarter and far more impressive – he could have done Wayne's job in a heartbeat.) The organisation was doing fantastically: financially successful and widely admired. Wayne was the star of the business community, receiving awards and accolades wherever he went, nominated to a bunch of federal government committees, and frequent lunch partner of several senior government ministers. Fittingly, Wayne lived in a big house in Mosman, one of Sydney's most affluent suburbs. He had a very, very nice car collection, and holidayed in the best locations.

Wayne worked hard, very hard. He spent at least twelve hours a day at work, often on the weekends as well. On three nights a week he had a work function, and if he wasn't in the office at the weekend he was playing golf with contacts or attending some work-related event. Wayne's message to his employees and the people he met was always laced with the ideas of focus and commitment. He loved the fact that his junior employees would pull all-nighters for the cause, to deliver a project or present a report. When the job was done, celebrations would be a big night out with his workers, who would join him rather than take the soft option and go home.

At the top of his game, Wayne oozed bravado, arrogance and power. When I first met him, we talked about the idea of a work–life balance, and Wayne's strongly held opinion was that balance was a personal issue, something that people should decide for themselves. In other words, if you don't have a balance between work and other parts of your life, then fine. I choose to focus on work, he said. That was undoubtedly true: even at the time, I knew that Wayne's personal life was a train wreck. He was on his second marriage and his relationship with his kids was pretty stormy. But his corporate profile was growing exponentially, and *that* was what was he was focusing on.

A couple of years later, Wayne left the CEO position in which he'd made his mark and went on to another company. This time he wasn't quite as successful, and suddenly there were critics where there had once been only fans. In his late fifties by then, he quit the job after two troubled years and began a non-executive career. He scored a few board positions but wielded nothing like the power that he had been used to. He was, of course, still very wealthy.

I met up with Wayne again a year or two back, at a presentation by the visiting CEO of a US technology company. Initially, he was just like old times – bluff, bravado and booming – but he was uncomfortable in the surroundings. He looked a bit like a fish out of water, in fact. After we'd discussed business and the economy for a while, he began to talk about himself. He talked about how his kids were both overseas and he never saw them. He was still with his second wife, but they were just cohabiting, really. There was no love left. His golfing friends had slowly moved away from him because, in his words, 'I am not able to help them with corporate influence and it seems I am no longer needed.' He still attended business functions, but it was quite clear that he didn't really know what his 'value add' was anymore. As the discussion progressed, Wayne became more and more open about the trajectory of his life and the big mistake he had made. Being a successful CEO had not been a mistake – that had been great. The mistake had been to let the power and wealth take him over and dominate his existence. He had begun to think that he was invincible. Now with twenty years or more left to live in his life, he couldn't see a happy or content future. He felt, he said, very lonely.

While we were chatting, some other guys came over to talk. As soon as Wayne spied them approaching, he changed suddenly and radically. Bluff, bravado and booming

Wayne returned, the arrogant and swashbuckling CEO incarnate. It was so obvious that this was a facade. I couldn't understand why he didn't see it himself.

A few months later I read an interview with him in the press, talking about his successful life. To my great annoyance he continued to perpetuate the myth that focused hard work and commitment will alone bring about fulfilment and success. Clearly he still didn't feel as if he could be honest and talk about the trade-offs that he had made. It was also annoying that the interviewer seemed prepared to accept Wayne's simplistic proposition: hard work = money = success = happiness.

David, on the other hand, never went for the glowing business magazine profiles, industry awards and accolades. He could have had them, I guess. His attitude to his career was perhaps best illustrated by his choice of golf club. David is a very good golfer and played every Saturday with friends for over twenty years. A member of one of the country's most prestigious clubs, he preferred to play at the Gordon public course – or 'Royal Gordon' as he would often describe it. This is good enough for me, he thought, and relinquished his exclusive club membership.

Up until his retirement about two years ago, he worked close to 9 to 5, and was home for dinner with his family at around 6 pm at least four nights out of five. He has always had a marvellously close relationship with his two children, who continue to ring him up most days for a chat. In retirement David keeps himself very busy, between Probis (a group of retirees that meets regularly), bowls, and seeing his friends and family. Everyone who meets him, without exception, comes away feeling warm towards him; and everyone who has known him is better off for the experience. He exudes a sense of happiness and contentment with his lot in life that is incredibly attractive – even if it wasn't to me twenty-odd years ago. As I now appreciate, David's most amazing characteristic is that he wants 'just enough'. Of course he wanted to live in a nice suburb, with a nice house and car, but he was able to turn off the desire for more and more, unlike Wayne, unlike Tim perhaps, and unlike most senior executives I meet.

Equally, David exhibits another characteristic that is rare among senior executives: A lack of bitterness or envy over the success of others. If you told David that one of his peers had just bought a new house, or a big boat, or had had a huge promotion, he would be genuinely pleased. (Mind you, as an avid golfer who has never hit a hole-in-one, he's devastated to hear of hackers knocking one in from the tee!) It is David's ability to keep everything in balance that defines him as one of the most successful men I have ever known. He aspired for sporting success as a child and did well. He aspired for career success and did well. He aspired for a great family and a group of good friends, and he has succeeded there also. His life is a success and one that many CEOs I know would love to trade their large houses, big boats, fast cars and telephone-number bank accounts for – happiness and contentment.

In a sense, David taught me one of the most valuable business lessons I have ever learned. Having initially written him off because of his seeming lack of ambition, I eventually came to see him as a very ambitious man because he wanted the best in *every* part of his life. He wanted a satisfying work life, but he also wanted a happy and stable home. He wanted the company of real friends, he wanted to be part of his community, and he wanted to be comfortable with his place in the world. At the end of his life, he can look back and say that he has been successful in all of these things.

As this book was being completed, David was diagnosed with terminal cancer and learned that he had months, rather than years, to live. It is a sad, difficult time in our family, but at the same time, David himself is a tower of strength. He is sad, but seems genuinely unafraid of dying. There is no sense of bitterness. Twenty-three years on from meeting him, my assessment of his achievements couldn't be more different.

I wouldn't wish it on anybody, but I can't help wondering how Wayne would react if he were told tomorrow that he had months to live. My guess is that his final months would be more about bitterness, a sense of loss for what has passed and been missed, and great sadness. In contrast, David has an underlying belief that he has lived a happy life the way he wanted. He has no regrets.

HOW TO READ THIS BOOK

This book is not for everyone. It is not for you if, on deep and honest reflection, you can say you are truly satisfied with your lot and the choices you have made. If you can say that you have a satisfying career, that you have the time you need to devote to your family, your friends and yourself, and that you have no regrets and feel you are truly living the life you want, then by all means put this book down. Likewise, if you have a clear view of what makes for a successful life and this definition has been tested with some rigour and has passed the test. If you can see your future as a time when your work, relationships and health are likely to blossom, leaving you at retirement with great contentment and happiness, then don't waste your time reading any more.

If, however, you are one of the 50 per cent of managers who work more than 50 hours per week, or are among the majority of mangers who name 'achieving a reasonable work–life balance' as their number one leadership challenge, then this book might have something for you. If you want to lead a truly successful life but are not quite sure how to frame such an idea – let alone structure a life plan to meet such a goal – then the following chapters may provide some help.

What Matters is intended to be a practical book. I have included ideas and tips to help people change their lives, as well as arguments to help you convince yourself and those around you that change is necessary. But to determine whether you want to make some change, let's begin with a practical exercise.

Take out a sheet of paper and draw a large circle on it. This circle is a pie chart representing your life and your priorities. Next you'll have to break this pie into slices that represent how important specific things are to you. Here are the names for each piece of the pie:

- Work
- Finances

- Spouse/partner
- Children
- Other family members
- Friends
- Hobbies/interests
- Community activities.

One second though. Before you start drawing on the pie there's another step. Just spend five minutes, with your eyes closed, in a quiet room, with no distractions, and think about the following scenario.

You have had a pain in your back but have been too busy to get to the doctor. Finally you see your GP, who on inspection asks you to have a pathology test. You do this (grudgingly, because this means more time out of your busy schedule) and a couple of days later your GP calls you to make a time to see him. Annoyed but also a little apprehensive, you meet the GP at 5.30 pm in his office. There you learn that you have an inoperable tumour in your spine that is a secondary cancer to one that is in your lungs (which explains the shortness of breath you have had recently). The tumour in your lungs is also inoper-able and sadly, even with the most aggressive treatments possible, your life expectancy is just six to twelve months. Stunned, you leave the surgery. You want a second opinion and embark on a journey of discovery to see what the options are.

A week later you have had two more opinions, both of which confirm the first diagnosis. You do indeed have six to twelve months to live. You have not told anyone else as yet but

*you are now leaving the doctor's surgery to go home and give
your family and friends the awful news. As you sit in the train
going home, you start to think about your life, how you have
spent the time, what you have focused on. On top of the obvious
distress at knowing that you will not be around for your
daughter's wedding or your son's graduation from uni or the
happy travelling days in retirement with your partner, are you
basically happy with how you spent your time or are you now
confronted with a horrible fact? That somehow, somewhere
along the road that is the journey of life, your priorities were
willingly hijacked and you ended up living a life for someone
else. This has not been a life that you would choose . . .*

Spend another five minutes with your eyes closed and think
about what matters in your life. You do not have a terminal
disease but you might one day. You do not have a six-month
life expectancy today but you will one day. You may not
reflect on how you are spending your life now but you will
then. Spend some time thinking about how you'll divide your
pie chart, the size of each segment being in proportion to how
much that segment means to you. You have to prioritise how
important each part of your life is to you, in other words.
(And it can't add up to more than 100 per cent or cover more
than one pie!) When you are ready, fill in the chart.

Now take a second sheet of paper and draw
another circle. This time the pie represents a normal month
of useful hours (ie when you are not sleeping, eating, having
a shower and so on). Let's be generous in time allocation and
assume fourteen hours a day. Using the same list as before,
break your pie into segments, each one being how much

time you actually spend on that activity or area in a typical month. This pie represents how you are living your life.

Now for the interesting part. Take each pie chart and put them side by side.

If, on comparison, you are spending 20 per cent of your time with family, and family represents 20 per cent of what matters to you, and if all segments are similarly aligned between what is important to you and how you spend your time, then a simple analysis would be that you are living your life in concert with what matters to you. If this is the case, you can stop reading now. Go play with your kids, go back to work and just continue living your life.

More likely perhaps, you'll find that some segments are not aligned. If, for example, you feel that your children are more important to you than the corresponding number of hours would suggest, or the whole thing is out of whack, then think about what this information means for you. If you take it seriously enough, the realisation might just be a life-changing insight.

Most people find that they spend far too much time at work relative to its importance to them, and are consequently short-changing the other things in their life. Their response is always along the lines of: 'Well, I have to work to keep the family going, so there's nothing I can do about it. Anyway, I can always catch up with the kids [spouse/family/friends/hobby etc] when work lightens up a bit . . .'

The first part of this answer is true: we all have to work to provide the financial stability for our lives and those of our family. The second and third parts are not true. To be specific, the 'I'll get around to it' bit is just wishful thinking, hoping that magically things will change. And the idea that nothing can be done about the situation is false. I am not saying that overnight you can make changes to completely align the pie charts, but you can start to take small steps that will gain momentum and ultimately deliver a situation where you are much closer to living the life you want to live.

I know people who have done some amazing things in their lives. They have competed in gruelling ironman events, scaled treacherous mountains, undertaken painstaking research projects – all activities that require focused effort and diligent application of time and energy. Before accepting that there is nothing that you can do, why not devote just some of the energy, drive, focus and intellect that we all have to the challenge of aligning your life with what you see as important. How can you maintain a fulfilling work life while also having enough time for the other things that matter? How can you build a life that meets your work aspirations (money, self-esteem, social network) and also lets you have energy and time to meet your other needs?

THE QUEST FOR A WORK–LIFE BALANCE

After spending almost 25 years in some of the most successful organisations in Australia, the USA, Europe and many parts of Asia, and having read a lot about efficient work environments, I know deep in my heart that the work environments in white-collar Australia are not always as efficient as they can be. The result is that rather than being focused on achieving our work goals in the minimum time (so that we can get back to other things in our life), we allocate all daylight hours (and more) to work, often with no regard to whether we will achieve the goals or not. This is a mad personification of the mouse on the treadmill – it is 'the rat race' after all – and in the end nobody wins. Equally true is the old adage that even if you win the rat race, you are still a rat.

The aim surely should be to achieve reasonable and challenging work goals while having time to live a full and happy life. When work takes up a reasonable chunk of our time, as it does, this can only happen if we focus on work efficiency and achieving sustainable goals, and not treating every day as a 100 metre sprint. Life is a marathon, not a sprint, and sustained effort leads to sustainable success.

Today work–life balance is not just a namby-pamby, soft and fluffy subject in the business world. It's the *number one* critical issue facing our organisations and the people within them. This fact is supported by a recent Mount Eliza Business School study, which surveyed 681 managers, 70 per cent of them men. The main issue on the agenda for these people was not how to make inroads into their markets or manage their people through uncertain times, it was how to achieve a reasonable work–life balance. The managers indicated that they felt they were working too many hours – between 51 and 55 hours a week, most of the men claimed – and that they were sacrificing the time that could be spent with their partners and children, or exercising or pursuing hobbies and interests. Only 2 per cent of those surveyed said they weren't making any sacrifices for their job.

What was especially interesting about the Mount Eliza results was the change from previous years. For every generation – from the Silent Generation (born in 1900–45) and the Baby Boomers (1946–54), to the Existentialists (1955–63), Generation Xers (1964–79) and Generation Yers (1980–88) – achieving a reasonable work–life balance was ranked first or second on the list of their concerns, up from fourth just two years ago.

The scary thing, then, is that the issue is becoming more urgent not less. But added to this is the very real threat of the ultimate in work–life *imbalance*, executive burnout. As noted in Mount Eliza's press release:

> *Commenting on the findings, Dr Karen Morley, Mt Eliza's general manager of design, development and delivery, said potential burn-out, as well as lack of energy, motivation and creativity among staff, raised serious questions about the real impact of work/life balance issues on business success.*
> *'Long hours are unsustainable. And they do not necessarily ensure that the right work is done,' Dr Morley said. 'Businesses also have to ask whether they are getting top performance in these conditions,' she added.*

Work–life balance is more than a personal issue. Managers are concerned about it not only because they feel a lack of balance in their own lives, but also because they can see the damage that our current overemphasis on work does to its role in our lives and its contribution to society. If we sacrifice our kids' childhoods on the altar of the office, how, exactly, have we become better off?

In material terms, we are better off today than we have ever been before, no question. Yet we see the decay of our society all around us – drugs and crime, the fragmentation of the family, a breakdown in values, increasing desperation and nihilism among the young, the dissipation of communities, social discord and conflict. If, as our politicians and business leaders would have us believe, economic growth alone is the answer to these problems, why have so many social indicators been getting worse while society itself has been getting 'richer'? It's enough to make people wonder what they're working for.

A BOOK IN THREE PARTS

What Matters is an exploration of these issues and what they mean for you. The book is divided into three sections. Part I recounts my own story, included because I think it is important for you the reader to understand where I am coming from and how I have come to my conclusions. My career has taken in periods of very long and satisfying work hours, and it has included successes as well as failures. But I have also had the privilege of working with and learning from some of the most amazing and successful people in the world.

Another reason for including my story is to justify my position, to some extent. Some people, hearing what my message is but not really listening, have an almost violent allergic reaction to what I am saying. 'It's alright for you,' they say, 'you've already *made* your money.' After many years in this game, I am practised at dealing with this objection, but I hope that by reading my story in detail and by understanding that my message might apply to your life as well as mine, this objection will seem less appropriate.

The second part of the book focuses on what the nature of real success might be, for the individual as well as for the corporation. Too often we assume that we know what success is: it's having a thriving business, making a lot of money, driving a flash car, living in a big house. Well, maybe. But surely the whole idea of success takes on a new light when you really sit down and think about it. (Think of David and Wayne.) Part II also contains some ideas about how business might begin to approach the issue of work–life balance, and how enlightened leadership will be the key to addressing this problem. The ideas draw from some of the work I have been doing with large Australian corporations.

The third part of the book attempts to provide you with some real strategies for dealing with the work–life balance issue in your own life. Like all change, it is difficult and complex, and we can use all the help we can get. I have asked experts on subjects such as money and health to provide some ideas for coming to grips with these things in our lives.

This book might not be for everyone. But if management school surveys and conversations with colleagues and dinner-party discussions can be relied on, I hope and expect that there might be something in it for a good number of people after all. My goal is to provide a catalyst for you to consider how you would define a successful life and how to create close alignment between the life you really want to lead and the one you may have ended up living.

In the end, it is all about regrets or a lack of them. It is about arriving in our latter years happy, content and feeling as though we have not only enjoyed the ride but have left behind tangible legacies in the relationships that define our lives. David motors on through chemotherapy, laughing about his hat choices now that his hair is falling out, sad about the fact that his innings will be more like a one-day game than a five-day test. Wayne has not been presented with a shorter innings and yet, because of the way he has led his life and the choices he has made, his journey is one of great sadness and bitterness.

Are you David or Wayne?

PART I

BUILDING SUSTAINABLE SUCCESS

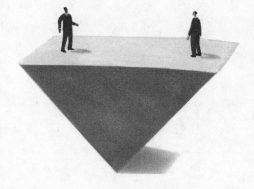

01

A SUCCESS STORY AND THEN …

It rains a lot in Washington state, in the north-western corner of the USA. Seattle, on the craggy shores of Puget Sound, is a famously wet city, but all that rain has a flipside: when the sun does come out, the colours are blinding. The city is surrounded by deep greens and autumnal reds and yellows, and beautiful, lush foliage of a kind that is foreign and startling to eyes that are used to the harsh craggy brown bushland that surrounds Sydney. The summertime climate in Washington is beautiful as well. Clear, crisp days with a lucid northern light that lasts well into the evening.

In summer 1992, at a place called Hood Canal, this was the magical backdrop for one of the more remarkable events in my professional career: a two-day executive strategy retreat at Bill Gates' summer holiday property with the top dozen executives at Microsoft.

Hood Canal is about 40 kilometres north of Seattle, along the shoreline of Puget Sound. Bill's property there is not flash. There are four houses – not mansions, just nice holiday houses on the lake – one for Bill and his family, one for his parents and one each for his sisters. The list of those present at the conference reads like a who's who of the computer industry: Bill himself, of course, in top form as usual; Steve Ballmer, passionate and zealous; Paul Allen, quiet, insular and smart; and a number of the long-time luminaries in the company such as Mike Maples, Brad Silverberg, Jeff Raikes, Pete Higgins, Jim Allchin and Paul Maritz. Many of these characters could have easily run any of the other major companies in the industry at the time, and were at worst peers to legends like Lou Gerstener at IBM or Steve Jobs and John Scully of Apple. For me, the fact that I was there at all, and for some of the time holding my own with the world's best, was pretty surreal.

Up for discussion at this retreat was the future of the world's fastest-growing and most exciting company, in the world's fastest-growing and most exciting industry: software. With Microsoft's top executives present, the sky was the limit. What companies should we buy? Should we be starting new divisions? Should we be investing in new areas? What were the competitive threats and how could we avoid having our ankles bitten by faster-moving companies?

At the time I was vice-president of the company's Workgroup Applications division, in charge of developing and marketing Microsoft's email and scheduling software (what we now know as Outlook and Exchange). We were coming from behind in the email battle and had a new competitor to deal with in the shape of Lotus Notes, a product that we simply did not have an answer for at the time. For all the challenges, it was the right place to be at the right time. Those familiar with the software industry will remember that in 1992, Microsoft had yet to commit to the internet, and that Notes was the dominant workgroup application. At this time, we knew that communications software was going to be immensely significant, but there were strategic issues around how Microsoft, as the industry leader, should approach the market.

Crucial issues for us, given the potential size of the market, were how to ensure we grew our market position in an exploding area and how to produce a solution that was better than our competitors'. For the world's leading software company, this was an immensely significant challenge, and I had been invited to make a presentation on these issues to the most critically challenging, enquiring and influential audience in the world: the full suite of Microsoft's senior executive talent. It was, to say the least, one of those pinch-yourself moments. This was the centre of the universe. As far as executive success is concerned, it just doesn't get any better than this, I thought.

TWO GOOD DECISIONS

I was appointed CEO of Microsoft Australia in July of 1988. That was clearly an achievement, but at the time it wasn't nearly as impressive as it would be today. Firstly, although Microsoft already dominated the market for operating systems with Windows and MS-DOS, it had yet to achieve its near monopoly status on the desktop. It had serious competitors in the word-processing and spreadsheet markets (Microsoft was running number two to Wordperfect, and number two to Lotus 1-2-3), and although the internet existed, email was very basic and proprietary. Surfing the web was a minority sport for computer dweebs.

Today, Microsoft Australia probably has a few hundred employees in the sales/marketing-focused entity, and if you counted its revenue correctly, it would turn over close to A$1 billion a year. Back in 1988, the company had about 30 staff covering everything from warehouse operations, technical support, sales, marketing and the rest, with an annual turnover of about A$12 million. There was clearly some growth to be had, and I took to the job with relish.

My appointment at Microsoft was the result of two good decisions taken earlier in my career. The first was to go into computing in the first place. When I left school, having failed to achieve my first two career choices – fighter pilot and doctor – I asked myself which industry was likely to make the most money. Given how things have changed and grown, going into computing was a good decision.

My second good decision was to get out of computing. Not out of computing altogether, but out of hardware. Some eleven years after beginning my career, I was national marketing manager at NEC, a company that sold a range of computers (from mainframes to PCs) and peripherals (printers, disk drives, etc) to the full range of clients from small business owners to large corporations. Over time it became clear to me that computer hardware was becoming a commodity product, where competition would do nothing but bring down prices and margins. No fun.

At about the same time, at age 28, I thought I ought to have a go at being a CEO. If I made it, I figured, that would be good; on the other hand, if I failed, I would quite happily go back to running a marketing group. I didn't think necessarily that I would be a good CEO but I was desperate to find out whether I could do the job or not. So two things were running around in my head: I wanted to get out of hardware, and I wanted to try my hand at running my own show.

Then the phone rang. On the other end was a head-hunter, Stuart Dredge at Intek, recruiting for the role of CEO of Microsoft Australia. If it sounds too good to be true now, it certainly felt like it then.

MEETING BILL

I didn't meet Bill Gates until some three months into my new job, but we hit it off immediately.

Forbes magazine calculated Gates' net worth in September 2003 to be US$46 billion. After Ingvar Kamprad, the founder of furniture chain Ikea, whose wealth is estimated by a Swedish business magazine at $53 billion, Gates is the richest man in the world by some $10 billion, way ahead of the next richest, Warren Buffett. Buffett, well into his seventies, is known as 'the Sage' for his wisdom. But let me assure you that William Henry Gates III equally deserves the label. He is far and away the cleverest person I have ever met, and it is difficult to overstate how stimulating it is to work with him. Constantly challenging and probing, his mind is both clear-thinking and nimble, somehow zeroing in on the core of the issue being discussed and turning it over until the solution, or a pathway to a potential solution, becomes clear.

And he is not just a computer geek. Of course Bill can easily tackle a technical discussion with any of his double-PhD brainbox computer scientists about the complexities of twenty-first century computing – he is, after all, still chief software architect of the software company to the world. And this depth of knowledge stretches across many other disciplines. One of the top US biotechnologists once told me that Bill Gates, who had just donated a large amount of funding to a research institute in the field, was one of the top three or four best-read people in the country in the area of biotechnology.

When I was running Microsoft's Workgroup Applications business, I was spending all day, every day, thinking about workgroup applications, about their development, competitive positioning, staffing, budgeting, and the myriad things that make up a business like that. And yet every conversation I had with Bill (a man who clearly had a lot more than workgroup applications on his mind) left me thinking, 'Wow, this guy is so far ahead of the game.'

More than that, even with this immense store of knowledge and the ability to manipulate it, he can still relate at the human level. I remember a presentation to analysts in New York, when he was being asked – as he is every day –

complex questions about his company and about the industry. One question was from a Wall Street analyst about the finer points of a particular part of Microsoft's balance sheet. Bill answered the question as asked, with the requisite amount of understanding and at the level of the enquirer. Ditto question two, from an IT journalist who asked about dynamic-linked libraries, a reasonably technical (in those days!) programming construct. Question three came from a *Wall Street Journal* writer, who wanted to know what an 'email front-end' was; a pushover for an über-tech like Bill, but he answered the query simply, with patience, and in a way that completely satisfied the person who had asked it. Bill's ability to relate is remarkable.

I attended many meetings between him and other industry legends and it is scary how much brighter he is than many of his direct competitors and partners. I think that much of Microsoft's success can be put down directly to Bill Gates' personality and intellect.

One of his most remarkable characteristics is his relative humility. Microsoft itself has never been accused of being particularly humble, but that is not the case with Gates. Clearly, the world's second richest man does not fit the classic definition of humble, but what sets Bill apart from many business leaders is his ability to listen to what is being said and adjust his thinking accordingly. When meeting with Bill, you have to have your data in order, you have to know what you are talking about and, importantly, you have to have thought through the consequences of your ideas. But if you've done all that, and you are right, Bill Gates will admit that he is wrong and let you run with the ball.

PROMOTION TO REDMOND

In late 1990, two years after my time with Microsoft began, Bill came down to Sydney for a meeting and asked me to move to Seattle. I declined. I felt there was a lot more for me to achieve in Australia. Less than twelve months later, however, Bill came back again and convinced me to take on what he said was one of the hardest jobs in the company – the Workgroup Applications division. Carolyn and I packed our bags and headed for Redmond, and I went to work on Microsoft campus.

Many factors contribute to Microsoft's success, but one of them is definitely its commitment to product development. The heart of Microsoft was and remains the product development group, and that is the way it should be.

Equally, however, Microsoft thinks through its marketing and positioning better than its competitors do. This period at Redmond taught me one important fact: it doesn't matter how much razzle dazzle you've got, you must also have a great product to sell and you need to invest serious IQ into your strategies.

There was no question that my commitment and dedication was paying off for me professionally. In late 1992, after I had been on campus for about eighteen months, I was in Bill's office discussing a number of very senior roles he was considering me for – promotion was around the corner. It was extremely exciting and I was eagerly awaiting a future dedicated to achieving great things on behalf of an employer that I loved. Still, there were already indications that I was not as single-mindedly committed to the cause as my other senior management colleagues. Being Australian, and only one of two non-American vice-presidents in the company, I was already different. But I was nicknamed 'the 9 to 5 VP' for insisting that I be able to go home to see my baby at least three evenings a week, and because I came in a little later in the mornings in order to spend some time with my family before work.

Before my first child, Grace, was born in 1989, one year after I joined Microsoft in Australia, I would easily work a 55-hour week. When I held her in my arms for the first time I was overwhelmed by the sense of responsibility, awe and love that she brought out in me, and I vowed that I would do everything I could to live up to the job of being her father. The first thing that meant, for me, was time: time to be with her and Carolyn. So I cut down my working hours to allow me to be with them before work, and before Grace went to sleep in the early evenings. Working 8 to 6, I felt, was surely enough to get done what needed to be done.

The birth of Grace created the beginnings of a seismic shift in my thinking about the balance between work and family. I started to think a lot about how to have an exciting career without sacrificing the rewards of a close family. Back in my days at Microsoft Australia we'd advocated that while we asked for dedication to the job, we understood that it is just that – a job. In retrospect and with almost fifteen years' more experience under my belt, I now realise there was a whole lot more we could have done to ensure that our people lived balanced lives. I mention this because many people say I was able to spend time with my baby because I was in the luxurious position of being CEO, and that option would not have been open to my employees. That is simply not true; the approach to work and life at Microsoft Australia was definitely different from Redmond.

QUANTITY VERSUS QUALITY

I had to make my time in the office consciously more productive as a result, but working at Microsoft Australia proved to me that if you had thought through the key business issues and you were focused on being time-efficient, there was no need to consistently work more than ten hours a day (no matter what your job was). I also knew from first-hand experience that if you do work more than ten hours a day (consistently), then your productivity declines rapidly and your health and relationships also suffer.

Microsoft is famous for the demands it makes of its people. The running joke was that if you worked at Microsoft, you only worked half time – you just had to decide which twelve hours of the day you wanted to work. The cafeteria was open 24-7-365. Douglas Copeland even wrote a novel, *Microserfs*, about the all-night coffee- and Coke-guzzling work sessions. And it is true, the company attracts remarkably dedicated and passionate people who often put their work before anything else in their lives.

THE DEATH MARCH

There are times in every company when long working hours and frantic schedules are unavoidable. In a Microsoft development group, the twelve weeks or so prior to a shipping date are those times. It is known as 'the death march'. On the shipping date, a new product is released to the market and hundreds of thousands of customers will flock to the stores (or online servers) to buy it; software reviewers will focus on nothing else, and the industry's eyes will be keenly-watching to see how Microsoft's latest offering will perform.

To correct any bugs in the product after the shipping date is enormously costly – tens of millions of dollars worth – and hugely humiliating for the company. If a bug is detected well before the shipping date, it costs nothing to fix, maybe just half an hour of a programmer's time; in the lead-up to shipping, however, things become a little more complicated. At death march time, more people are involved, the ramifications of changes are larger, and stress levels are high. Yet all bugs need to be corrected, of course. There is constant conflict between the developers, who are the group's backbone, and the testers, who check their work. When bugs are found this late in production, accusations fly and blame is rife. People are tired and tetchy, as most are pulling sixteen- to eighteen-hour days, and many of them don't even go home. The strains on relations inevitably show.

My job as leader of the group was mostly to get in between and calm people down, manage expectations and processes, and generally keep the project on the rails. In a sense you are the triage guy, who makes assessments of situations and prioritises. You make sure your people don't kill each other and remind them that, after all, it's only software.

At these times I would also be working long hours – it was simply the nature of the position. How, you may ask, did this sit with my work–life balance approach? Under these circumstances, all you can do is remember that products ship only every couple of years, and that the deadline date is a full stop to these working patterns. It is all too easy to get caught up in the momentum and begin to mistake the emergency-deadline work mode for the every day.

Still, apart from during the death marches, in Redmond my approach to work was different from that of the hardcore Microserfs depicted by Douglas Copeland. I always tried to impress that it is impossible to work hard but also have a life outside the workplace. I did not accept that we had to trade business success for a balanced life, but rather we had to be very focused on doing the right things at the right time and also understand that just running faster (or working more hours) will not produce business success. Despite my noticeably different attitude to working hours, the group I ran was doing very well. Revenue, profit and market share were all up significantly, and – the best test – Bill was very pleased with our progress.

On top of this excellent performance, I would receive many emails from my employees' partners thanking me for being the first senior executive at the company to realise that Microsoft employees had families as well. At the same time though, I was the butt of many jokes within the ranks of senior management for being the so-called part-time VP.

It seemed that to challenge the 'all or nothing' mantra was some form of disloyalty and implied that I lacked drive. Neither was the case. I just had a deep belief that if you kept things in perspective and applied intellect and energy, you could balance the competing needs and develop a successful, balanced life.

A NEW PERSPECTIVE

Very late one evening in December 1992, my mother telephoned from Australia with some very bad news. My sister, Gabriela, whom I loved dearly, had been killed in a car crash driving between Young and Canberra. She left behind a badly injured baby girl and her husband, who was also injured.

It was so unfair, so wrong. Gabriela had had a tough time during adolescence, having developed anorexia in her teens, and her life was just beginning to normalise. She had a stellar career, had recently got married, and now had a baby to complete the picture. Her entry into parenthood had given us some common ground, and we'd just started talking about things and building a new friendship. Then she was simply not there anymore. This was an event that shattered my entire perspective on life.

In the workplace, surrounded by the support network provided by the corporation and the symbols of our position, you can be the master of your own domain. Things go wrong, mistakes are made, people let you down, yes, but all of this happens within an accepted framework. Decisions are made in a particular way, and communicated and executed with varying levels of success, and in the end we understand that the workplace demands a particular type of interaction and follows specific rules. But the death of a loved one falls outside the bounds of such networks, frameworks and rules.

When Gabriela was killed, it revealed to me that I'd been labouring under the illusion that life is as controllable as events in the workplace. To have something so valuable taken away without any warning, without any discussion or workshopping or decision-making processes, to be unable to exchange any of the tokens of my success for something as simple as a telephone call or a cup of coffee with my sister, was truly traumatising. If all of the power, money and professional respect I had built up over the previous thirteen years amounted to less than that, what exactly was I working flat chat for?

Within hours I had decided that my approach to life had to change and we decided to return to Australia. My parents, my brother-in-law and my niece needed my wife and me, and that was what mattered.

The day after my mother's phone call, I spoke to Bill and told him that we had to go home, that I was needed elsewhere more than I was needed in Redmond. He was totally understanding, and in fact decided to move the Asia–Pacific headquarters of Microsoft from Seattle to Sydney. This was a complex decision for him, and, I am sure, not one that he would have taken had he not been convinced that it was the right thing to do for the company as well as for me. I was immensely lucky, and very grateful that I had such an understanding and forward-thinking employer. My good fortune aside, it did emphasise to me how important it is for companies to understand that their people are just that, *people*, with lives and problems of their own, and that this is not necessarily a bad thing. After all, the corporation can benefit in the long term by being loyal to its people and making adjustments.

If Gabriela was still alive, I have no doubt that we would have stayed in Redmond for several more years. I was thoroughly enjoying my work and was looking forward to a bright future with Microsoft. Carolyn and I had always intended to come back to Australia to bring up the children, but with our two girls years away from starting school, that decision was a while away yet, and who knows what might have happened in the meantime.

Those plans changed fundamentally with the news. Up until then, I'd felt as if I was climbing a mountain, nearing the summit with my eyes fixed on the top. But my sister's death forced me to sit down and rest; I looked around at the view and decided that it was just fine from where I was. Attending Hood Canal retreats and being within the inner sanctum of one of the world's greatest corporations, and everything that went with it, was remarkable, but not all that I wanted in life – I didn't need to climb the rest of the way.

A HOLISTIC VIEW OF WORK AND LIFE

Parenting psychologists say there are three types of parent. The first type, about 10 per cent of parents, had a marvellous childhood, full of magical, special days and laughter, and they remember it and make a conscious effort to re-create that for their own children. A further 10 per cent of parents had a ghastly childhood, full of fear, pain and confusion. They too remember it and consciously decide to avoid creating the same kind of atmosphere for their children. The third type of parent, into which the remaining 80 per cent of us fall, had a reasonable childhood, neither particularly magical nor particularly painful, and take the same kind of approach to their own parenting.

Translating those categories of past experience into the business world, I was the second type of parent. My childhood, that is my early employment history, provided me with bosses that were unfortunate role models. Textbook type-A personalities, they were aggressive and macho, hard-edged and unforgiving. Business decisions were right or wrong – nothing in between – people were to be praised or blamed, the office environment was fraught with aggressive politics, and the dominant emotion was anger. A few months into my job at NEC I went to the dentist because I was grinding my teeth at night. He gave me a plate to put in my mouth to treat the symptoms, but the cause of my grinding was the environment in which I was working. Every day we would have meetings with people screaming at each other, and the political infighting was vicious. This, after all, was 1980s Australian business culture.

Although I knew I disliked it, I didn't have the maturity or wisdom to know (at that time) whether my opinion of a healthy work environment was an accurate one or not. Still, I had a strong feeling that there had to be a better way to create successful organisations. When I was appointed CEO at Microsoft Australia I decided to consciously seek out another way. I thought a lot about creating a constructive environment for people to work in, one in which we would work hard because we wanted to and were driven to succeed, not because we were fearful or vengeful. I also began thinking and talking about how to balance the needs of the business with the broader needs of its people, how time in the office is worthless if it doesn't produce performance, and how the performance of a company is directly linked to the morale of its people. My thoughts were unformed as there was little literature on the subject – and the concept of work–life balance hadn't even been invented. I was groping in the dark but the seeds were there even from the beginning.

When I came back to Sydney in December 1993, I had a mission, to perform my job as well as possible, but also to be as rounded a person as I could: to be a good father and husband, to become an active member of my local community, and to develop some real friendships. I objected to the false mutual exclusivity between the role of hard-nosed 'successful' executive and one's duty as a human being. Surely, I felt, it is possible to be both (and then some). I began to cast around for a broader definition of success than the one I had been working to all those years. The results of my exploration appear later in this book, in Part II.

Once back in Australia I dedicated my energies to ensuring that my life was as balanced as possible across all its facets. This did not mean I would stop working – in fact, if you include my formal work hours and the hours I spend on various government committees, corporate and hospital boards, I am actually 'working' more hours now than before. But I knew that by focusing on getting things done and fitting things in, I could balance all the things that I wanted to.

The underlying tenets of my strategy were as follows:
1. *Understand what really matters to me.* This was not obvious or easy, and took time and energy. The last part of this book is dedicated to providing some practical suggestions for doing this.

2. *Work out how to do my job in the most efficient and pro-ductive way.* I made very sure that my time at work was as efficient as it could be. I developed the ability to say no to meetings and functions I felt would be of little value. I did not attend business lunches (a cup of coffee can achieve the same impact on client relationships), I did not hang around the office, and I did not engage in discussions or activities that were not part of creating a successful business. Most work environments create unnecessary activities not related in any way to the objec-tives of the business.

3. *Allocate time to the other things in my life.* I became ruthless with my diary.

4. *Do not look for acceptance from some work colleagues.* They simply did not yet 'get it', I reasoned.

SLEDGED

Some ten years on from that original decision to come back to Australia and lead a more balanced life, I continue to feel ostracised by the executive world that has been my work home for over twenty years. To be honest, I'm treated as some hippy-dippy weirdo. All I have done of course is cut back my working hours to something resembling normal, and proselytise the importance of family life.

People responded aggressively to my initial decision to quit the fast track, but the real sledging was saved for after my first book, *Father Time*, was published in 1998. *Father Time* had a simple message: people who have taken the decision to become fathers should be fathers. This means they should spend *real* time with their children, not 'quality' time. They should make simple arrangements that would allow them to be home to see their kids for dinner and bedtime, say, three times a week; they should try to not work on the weekends; they should go to school with their kids for a morning, maybe once a term. In short, they should prioritise their family over their work simply because it *is* more important.

Frankly I thought this was pretty uncontroversial stuff. How wrong I was.

A TYPICAL WORK DO

After the publication of *Father Time*, it was open season on Petre. I remember at one work function, a large, aggressive man, the managing partner of a law firm, stormed up to me, on the attack.

'You don't understand,' he told me. 'All this family-time stuff is bullshit.'

Nowadays I am well practised at dealing with such encounters, but back then I was regularly taken aback.

'Pardon?' I said.

'You don't understand the responsibilities I shoulder. You don't understand how much I am needed. I can't just go fishing with my son . . .'

'So you don't have any discretionary time? Everything you do at work is *essential*?' I asked.

'Crises pop up all the time. If I am not there, things will go out of control.'

'Do you ever do a corporate lunch?'

'That is a crucial part of doing business in my game. It's about developing relationships and making connections.' His face was getting redder now.

'Do you ever do a corporate golf day?'

'Of course I do. How else do you get to know people and find out what's going on in the industry?' Flecks of spittle were beginning to spray from his mouth.

'Come on,' I said. 'We both know that those activities are not 100 per cent productive, and that they use up a lot of time to achieve not very much.'

And that's when he lost his temper.

My biggest problem with this kind of conversation is that he was simply not being honest with himself, and got angry with me because I had touched a raw nerve. I have no issue with the executive who admits that he would rather be in the office or on a corporate golf day. It is the hypocrisy of claiming that he'd rather be with his family while *choosing* to be at golf that grates with me.

After *Father Time*, there were two types of reaction to my position. The first often came from the partners of executives, or those executives who understood what I was saying, and was one of gratitude and understanding. Many people sent letters saying that they were distressed because they couldn't control their own time, and were missing out on their children's lives; many were angry at the anti-family environment in their companies; and many told me how they had already lost touch with their children and thanked me for bringing the issue to public attention.

The other reaction was perhaps more typical. In short, I was made to feel like the guy who came back from the rugby tour and told the women what had gone on. I became a public target for every dissatisfied corporate executive with high blood pressure. At work engagements or dinner parties, in correspondence about *Father Time*, and in the many conversations I had about the book with others, people would attack me, telling me that I was making outlandish and outrageous claims. They would list reasons why they couldn't possibly do what I was saying.

These responses completely dumbfounded me. I understand that the corporate environment promotes certain values and that people tend to react negatively to anything that might challenge the status quo. At Microsoft, the birthplace of the 27-hour day, it was reasonably clear why people criticised my decision to quit my VP position and return to Australia. For many, my decision confronted the fundamental premise that formed the foundation of the modern career: the only way is up. Any downward or lateral move in the corporate hierarchy – even if it's taken for the valid reason of wanting to spend more time with one's family – is deemed a failure. The reaction initially within Microsoft was really puzzling to me. I never expected people to applaud my decision, but I hoped they'd at least respect it and work with me the same as they had before. But this was not the case and it's still not.

The barbs from my colleagues used to upset me, but now I see them in the context of the following quote from Arthur Schopenhauer:

All truth passes through three stages.

First, it is ridiculed.

Second, it is violently opposed.

Third, it is accepted as being self-evident.

SOME LESSONS FROM MY EARLY CAREER

You need to spend time and effort on strategy and you need to communicate this effectively.

- You need a clear vision of where you want to be and you have to engender support from your staff for this vision.
- You need to be honest about where your industry is heading and what the trends will be.
- Invest in the future – not in a random way but in a clear, measurable, programmed way. The future will be today very soon!
- Understand your market and your competitors.
- Be honest about your market position and service/product offering.
- Have a realistic, programmed plan that you can track and that has clear parameters for both the business and the health of employees.
- The strategy document must be a living document not some tome created and put on the shelf.

You need clear measures that you reference every month, quarter and year:

- Not just financials as these can disguise issues.

- Track also market share, unit sales, unit costs, competitive metrics, etc.

Mistakes are okay.

- If you have really planned something well and everybody has agreed with the plan but something goes wrong, looking for a scapegoat is the *wrong* approach. You need the maturity to see what went wrong and where the plan was wrong. (Did we underestimate the competition? Did we overestimate our ability to execute?)
- If you have spent the time on planning, there will always be an effective plan B option.
- Beware the CEO who looks for someone to blame when things go wrong (and beware of becoming that type of leader yourself). This immature approach motivates people to either hide mistakes or try to apportion blame to others. The culture that develops is not one focused on moving forward but on protecting your back – an incredible waste of time and energy.

Make sure your product/service offering is the best it can be. Understand that the soul of your company is the group that produces the product/service offering.

02

FROM ECORP TO SUSTAINABLE SUCCESS

In my working career I have been fortunate enough to work closely with two of the world's most successful businessmen. My early career was shaped and influenced by Bill Gates, the richest man in the USA. Later, I was able to work with the richest man in Australia, Kerry Packer. Both men taught me great business lessons. But they also taught me, intentionally and unintentionally, a great deal about the true nature of success.

ECORP

After nearly four frantic and successful years back in Australia running Microsoft Asia Pacific, I decided it was time to move on. I had thoroughly enjoyed my time at Microsoft but wanted to have more life and career experiences. In 1997, the internet was still in its commercial infancy. Many companies knew it was going to be immensely influential, but not many knew how they could exploit it to their advantage.

Publishing and Broadcasting Limited (PBL), Kerry Packer's company run by his son James, was casting around for a strategy that would enable it to profitably transfer some of its traditional media content and quality brands (Channel 9, *Women's Weekly*, *Bulletin* and many others) to the online world. Later I heard that in a conversation with Microsoft's Steve Ballmer, James had asked who might lead such a project, and Ballmer mentioned my name. At the time I was having many conversations about the exciting things that could be done with the web, so I was not surprised to receive an invitation from James and Kerry to dinner at a restaurant in Surry Hills in Sydney. It was clear they were recruiting.

I was very impressed by James Packer, even at that first meeting. He was savvy enough to realise that the media landscape was changing and that PBL needed to leverage its content on the web. And Kerry was very keen to do something based in Australia that was as good as anything in the world. That night I told them I thought the internet would be about applying the best technology on offer and pushing it with good old marketing leverage.

PBL is a world-class marketing engine. Success on the web would mean either investing massively in R&D or importing the world's best technology as cheaply as possible and marketing it through the company's traditional channels. Competitors who didn't have the technology or who were unable to market it would fail. I thought PBL could establish an internet operation with A$20–30 million, which would involve investing in some high-risk projects. Some would come a cropper (and some did) but there might be a few big winners.

The Packers offered me a job and asked me what position I would like to take on. As I was heavily committed to study, my family and to board positions with other organisations, I didn't want a full-time executive position, so I proposed that I take on an executive chairman position, three days a week. I would work closely with the CEO of each of ecorp's ventures, and I would have two days a week to give to other commitments. I still wasn't working part-time, of course. My working week was full, but it was made up of a variety of activities that brought me different satisfactions.

THE TRUTH ABOUT ECORP

In establishing the company, ecorp's co-founder and deputy executive chairman Jeremy Philips and I proceeded to implement the strategy I'd outlined to the Packers: by joint-venturing the best technology in the world with PBL's marketing might, we would have a winner. Ecorp's classic successes eBay and ninemsn (Microsoft's internet technology joint-ventured with the Nine Network) illustrate this perfectly. The joint-venture strategy was high risk, but this was a new world order and everyone was throwing huge amounts of money at the opportunities.

Ecorp started with $30 million in PBL cash and we also bought Ticketek for $50 million that first year from CPH. Jeremy and I worked out that the key places that were going to be huge businesses were, in order: internal portals; auctions; ticketing; financial services; and job classifieds. It surprised us that our competitors at Fairfax, News Ltd and Telstra hadn't come to a similar conclusion. They all tried parts of this but never really worked out that success on the internet was an 'and' function – world-class technology *and* low-cost/high-impact marketing leverage. It also surprised us that both Fairfax and News failed to understand that the internet was going to change the economic and business models of many industries.

Having put in an initial investment of $30 million plus the acquisition of Ticketek, the Packers floated ecorp in 1999 for just over A$800 million. Over the next couple of years we focused on trying to make our businesses a success. Meanwhile the markets went nuts. Ecorp at its highest had a market capitalisation of $4.8 billion, and even after the bubble burst, ecorp at its lowest was valued at just under $200 million. Quite a ride, throughout which neither PBL, Jeremy or I sold any of our shares as we remained focused on building great businesses.

Not all of our ideas came to fruition, however, and we had a couple of investment failures. The Charles Schwab venture went sour because we took too long to launch the business and then failed to ensure that the business stayed focused on the right issues. We also had less than stellar success with Monster.com. Balancing this, in the portal space, ninemsn was the outright leader, and remains so, even though Telstra and Fairfax have spent significantly more money than ecorp in this market. Ninemsn is now profitable (as we said it would be in year four).

In the auction space, the eBay venture was a stand-out success: $6 million invested in 1999 turned into a $120 million profit in 2002. This was the result of the right business decision but also by having an outstanding CEO in Alison Deans. Alison went on to become CEO of ecorp and she will, if she so chooses, go on to become one of the most influential female executives in Australia – such are her skills and attitude. Ebay continues to be a great success story, likewise our second financial services play, Wizard, and Ticketek.

PBL decided to buy back ecorp in early 2003, when the markets were depressed by the fear of recession in the USA. Added to that, the Iraq war was making everybody nervous and no one was investing in anything. Technology stocks languished, but very soon after, the markets would begin to turn up. PBL bought back ecorp at the bargain price of 55 cents a share – having floated it at $1.20 just four years earlier. At the time of the buyback, ecorp had approximately $150 million in cash, and the losses in the start-ups (ninemsn and the others) had all narrowed dramatically as they started to gain their market leverage. The operational engines had turned. Within twelve months ecorp would turn in a group profit, just one year later than we had projected at the time of the float, before the bubble burst.

Kerry Packer is famous for doing some of the best deals in Australian business history – most notably selling Channel 9 to Alan Bond for $1 billion, and then taking it back from him not eighteen months later in exchange for a sub-$200 million debt Bond owed from the time of the deal. The timing of the ecorp deal again showcased Packer's brilliance in this area. Since PBL bought back ecorp, the broad technology comparables have all grown considerably (Yahoo, for instance, is up over 300 per cent over the period from the date of the ecorp buyback to now), as has the performance of the ecorp companies.

KERRY AND JAMES PACKER – A STUDY IN CONTRASTS?

As well as his remarkable sense of business timing, Kerry Packer has a very good business intuition and a strong talent for knowing what will work, especially in television. He is undeniably tenacious, aggressive and driven. His temper is legendary and his comportment in business meetings is every bit as unsettling as the myriad of Kerry legends suggest.

On the other hand, James Packer is a much more relaxed and relationship-focused personality. His style is far more engaging – he wants people to get excited about doing things together – and it is James's style that is making PBL a success today. Much of PBL's current growth and direction is being achieved in new areas that were James's initiative, including the internet, Foxtel, Crown, and financial services.

James Packer's most significant corporate failure, OneTel, exposes the best and the worst of his business style. It was a bold move into a new and potentially very profitable industry: telecoms. It was a solid business model, a strong brand and an audacious play. And he trusted his management to deliver on their promises. Only in this case he trusted the wrong people – they overreached and were underskilled, and perhaps weren't monitored effectively, and the result was a train wreck. James is a very trusting person, but with OneTel his trust was misplaced.

PBL's other new ventures have all been instigated by James, and together they have made a lot more money than OneTel lost, so even at this stage of his career, his investment P&L (profit and loss) is strongly in the black. Many people think that today's PBL is driven by Kerry, and that it was Packer senior who rode back into town to save the company. This is not quite true, however. Kerry's presence focuses PBL executives, but it is equally fair to say that the underlying strategy that is producing success at PBL was developed and instigated by James. Kerry, of course, continues to add incredible value to the television and magazine businesses. The current success of PBL, then, is a combination of the vision of James and the television genius of Kerry.

SUSTAINABLE LEADERSHIP

I told Kerry and James that I would work with ecorp for five years, and that is what I did. I left the company to dedicate myself to promoting the idea of the sustainable organisation, and started up a consultancy designed to promote balance in corporate life. As stated in the previous chapter, when I started as CEO at Microsoft Australia, I wanted to actively create a more positive work culture and a balance between work and life for our people. My work now is a continuation of that project, attempting to take this philosophy into other organisations, and convert other business leaders to the cause.

Over time, the scope of my work has developed, and recently my business was merged into the People, Culture and Performance practice at Pricewaterhouse-Coopers. This move has created an opportunity to develop a service that can focus on leadership and organisational cultural development, along with the hard services of reward planning and organisational effectiveness strategies. In this way PricewaterhouseCoopers now assists major corporations in establishing businesses that are sustainably successful, delivering both increased productivity as well as increased employee engagement and satisfaction.

For me, the culture of obsessive focus on work and long working hours is a symptom of many things that are wrong with the way we run our businesses in Australia. The issue of work–life balance is symbolic of a short-termism in Australian business culture, which directly leads to many of the events that dominate the business pages: fraud, collapses, governance scandals and the like.

Just consider how familiar the following scenario is. A CEO has come into a company with a mandate for change. He works obsessively long hours and is brutal in cutting back costs. Strategy is overhauled, and the structures and knowledge that have been built up over years are destroyed. As a result, short-term profitability goes up and the CEO makes his bonus. After three years he parachutes out with a multi-million-dollar pay-off. Meanwhile his people have been through their umpteenth reorganisation and have been forced through goodness knows how many 'death marches' to make near-impossible deadlines. They're left holding together an organisation that the (now unaccountable) CEO has ravaged.

All the research shows that in organisations, culture is everything. And culture is set and determined from the top: the chief executive. So, it's down to perhaps 500 people, mostly men, who are at the top of the country's biggest companies – they're the cause of the problem. If these people were to realise that their role in life was to encourage something other than an unhealthy focus on long hours and the short-term perspective, it would amount to a revolution in society, one that would change things very much for the better.

For a company to deliver sustained performance, it needs to have a culture that attracts, retains and develops talent. Increasingly this will mean providing people with challenging jobs but also letting them have a life outside the workplace. A company's key asset is its people, after all, and the key to success will be developing loyalty over the longer term. This is not some two-year plan, it is a ten-year issue. From first-hand experience, I know that this is going to be a huge influence on the organisations of tomorrow.

THE GENERATION GAP

During a recent workshop session at a law firm, there was a stark contrast in attitude between the senior management and the junior partners coming up through the ranks.

The focus of senior management, led by the managing partner, was on how to increase billable hours from each employee and maximise partners' remuneration packages. That, they felt, was the key to attracting and retaining talent.

When given a chance to speak, the junior partners were forthright. 'We don't want more money,' said one. 'We've got enough. What we want is more freedom and time.' Another said: 'My father was a partner is a law firm, and I saw how dysfunctional and lonely his life became. I don't want to be like him.'

After the workshop I spoke to the managing partner about it.

'Oh,' he said, 'they don't really mean it.'

Could it be any more obvious that the younger generation has a different view from the older one on what constitutes corporate leadership?

This is not as easy or glib a transformation as it sounds. Today's generation of CEOs were bred in an era of intense internal competition. They are habitually on guard and create a facade of 100 per cent focused performance. Many feel that their lives are synonymous with the companies they work for; they have 'sold their souls' and thus do not have a right to expect any more from life. These leaders sacrifice all meaningful relationships on a false altar of success and believe that the rewards provided by the business environment ought to be enough.

What is ironic is that this is the very attitude that causes dysfunction within the organisation. With the CEO setting such a poor example, the rest of the organisation follows suit, and longer-term performance suffers.

My recent work focused on the belief that if you can motivate CEOs to exhibit more normalised human behaviour, their organisations will perform better. Everything then, from the work life of the CEO and those on the factory floor through to the company's financial performance, will improve.

It is not an easy task. To take a senior executive to a place where they can admit their fears, failings, insecurity and humanity is a complex task. They feel uncomfortable and exposed, and the process can be very confronting. But it can be exceptionally rewarding for the individual as well as the company they run.

COACHING FOR SUSTAINABLE LEADERSHIP

Over the last year I have been working with the CEO of a large Australian company. My original brief was to provide executive coaching as he was struggling with some business issues. After I'd spent some time with the CEO, however, it became clear that while he was a very smart and successful business person, he had not developed a very effective leadership style. Every key decision he felt he alone had to make, and there was little true debate in management meetings. And most importantly, the business was stagnating.

My initial focus was on developing a diagnostic of the leadership team's culture and presenting this to the CEO. What we found (not surprisingly) was that the others in the leadership team were fearful of the CEO, they did not trust each other, they were risk-adverse, and while they respected the CEO's intellect, they found his management style bordering on abusive. The CEO found the feedback quite disturbing, but to his credit, he engaged in a series of discussions and workshops (both personally and with his team) to develop a better relationship with them and to develop a more positive leadership style. The catalyst was the feedback, and it was powerful because many CEOs have very low levels of self-awareness – they are often quite ignorant of the impact of their behaviour.

Twelve months on, the business is in better shape (higher revenue growth, more profitable), the leadership team feels more engaged, positive and fulfilled in their respective roles, and the CEO now confides that he is much happier in this new style of leadership. He actually believes it is a style that is more aligned with his personal values than before.

As my career has moved from being fully focused as a CEO to having a portfolio of roles and responsibilities, I have found it somewhat easier to attain my goal of a balanced and well-structured life. I work as hard now as I ever did, but my time is split into a series of challenges, from private equity investment management and consulting, to sitting on community and school boards, and running Dad's Canteen at my children's school.

LESSONS ON PROFESSIONAL AND ORGANISATIONAL BALANCE

Leadership

Work in a company and industry that you feel passionate about. If you are really engaged and care about what you are doing you will be more successful and you will enjoy yourself more.

Leaders need to:

- Have a high IQ. For all the bluff and bluster about 'can do' people, CEOs need to be able to deal with complex problems and keep track of lots of issues. They need the intellectual capacity to make good decisions in a difficult environment.

- Be humble. Realise that you are very lucky to have your role, and that chances are, you are actually not much smarter or more skilled than many other people in your company.

- Have real empathy for others. Realise that most staff will not be able to retire early; they want to work hard but to also have a strong family life.

- Be good communicators at all levels, from board members and senior managers, down to entry-level people.

- Be open to criticism. Solicit this from all areas and take it on board – do not rationalise it away.

- Be focused on the long-term benefits for both shareholders and employees.

- Understand that commitment is not about working harder but about working smarter to meet goals that are sustainable over the long term. This is a marathon not a never-ending set of sprints.

Wherever you are on the corporate ladder, you do not have permission to be rude, aggressive or dismissive of anyone else.

Personal Lessons
- Life is very short. Do not die wondering what could have been, or with regrets.
- The love of a friend, wife or child matters more than a new car or other appliance.
- Do not assume that financial achievements will bring with them happiness. Financial success brings choice (which in itself is a great gift) but it is how you exercise choice that will determine your true level of happiness. If you want to have it all, then learn to compromise but don't just compromise everything to support your work.
- Happiness is about far more than working. Studies show that the happiest people are not those that have retired wealthy but those that have fulfilling jobs *and* the ability and resources to develop deep family and friend relationships (among other things).
- The people that can make a material change to all our lives are the chief executives of the top 500 companies and government organisations. It is the CEO that sets the culture, allows people to focus on productivity and efficiency as opposed to work hours.

PART II

SUCCESS AND LEADERSHIP

03

WORK AND LIFE

We build great industrial corporations which introduce amazing novelties into life. Their executives behave first, last and nearly all the time as if their companies had no function except to manufacture and sell. They have a fine understanding of their own business, too little grasp of their industries as a whole, almost none of the relation between particular interests and our general social and economic structure, and far too little grip on the social consequences of their activities . . .

WALLACE B. DONHAM, *HARVARD BUSINESS REVIEW*, JULY 1933

The other day I was in a lift in the city, heading up to a meeting with a CEO client. In the lift with me were two young women executives, talking about a third – let's call her Sam. Sam, it seems, had had a baby just three weeks earlier and was now back at work full time.

What struck me about this exchange was that these women were speaking of their colleague in tones of reverence, as if she had done something amazing by coming back to the office so soon. Sam's commitment to the company was awesome, they seemed to be saying. For me this is a remarkable shift. Think of Sam, the woman who has come back to work. Given the choice between a once-in-a-lifetime experience of physically being there during the first few months of her child's life, and helping her corporate clients achieve their quarterly targets, Sam had chosen the latter. Not only that, but the women with whom she works applaud her choice.

This conversation reveals a number of things about the modern working world. Firstly, it is fantastic that this choice is even available to Sam and her partner. Her partner, I was told, has been granted paternity leave (paid!) to raise the baby, so the mother takes the breadwinner role while the father is primary caregiver. This arrangement is rare enough today, but was almost unheard of even ten years ago. It's a marvellous development in life choice for both the woman and the man, and represents a quantum leap in the ability of people to live the lives they want to.

The second thing it reveals is that when we are given choices, we seem to have a tendency to make the wrong ones. Far be it from me to speak for Sam. She may live for work and enjoy it so much that to be away from it with her newborn baby for a couple of months, six weeks, a month even, would be difficult. As I said, it is great that she is *able* to come back to work after three weeks if she chooses to. But the organisation she works for offers all female staff generous paid maternity leave; therefore, in this situation, both the mother and the father could have stayed at home with the baby for the first few months while still drawing very similar salaries. Within this framework I find Sam's decision intriguing, to say the least.

Equally, I find it distressing to hear of organisations that offer paid paternity leave for fathers – often for around six weeks – but have very few fathers taking up the option at any stage during the first year of their child's life (the period during which most paternity leave is offered). Your baby goes through many stages, each one lasting longer than the previous one. They are a child, then an adolescent for a number of years, a young adult for longer, and an adult for a long time. They are, however, a newborn baby for a very short time.

I have a hard time believing that whatever was going on at Sam's city firm that week was more important than what was happening at home. And I can't understand how her colleagues in the lift – or anyone else who knew of Sam's decision, male or female – thought that any workplace event could be more important than what was happening in Sam's home. I am not suggesting Sam should have given up her career. As the father of three girls I want them to have a family and a career. I do think, however, that Sam could have taken a few months off to bond with her child.

THE GREAT TRADE-OFF

Life is a series of decisions and choices. To have breakfast or not. To wear a suit or pants and a shirt. To take a particular job or not. Even not making a decision can be a decision.

And the heartbreaking thing about it is that every decision is a trade-off. You can't have breakfast and not have breakfast, or wear the suit and the pants and shirt (well, I suppose you could, but you'd look a bit strange). And you can't dedicate every waking hour of your day for the bulk of your life to work *and* have a sustainably successful life.

But, and this is the key to my message, you *can* be a success at work – achieve things, be respected, have an interesting and rewarding career – without dedicating every waking hour of the day for the bulk of your life to it. A sustainably successful life is one that puts as much passion into all parts of the person, not simply the work life. It takes planning, effort and an understanding of the nature of the trade-offs that you are making when you make your life decisions.

I think of the many men I know who have sacrificed their family lives for the sake of the office. Those that spent so many early mornings, late nights and weekends in the office that their families grew away from them. When it is too late, and they realise what has happened, they bitterly regret their decisions. But often this regret is inevitable because throughout their lives they have made life decisions without even recognising them as such. Every weekend on Saturday, for instance, instead of consciously making the decision to fertilise family relationships, they would decide to play golf with work buddies or go in to the office. At the time, it simply seemed like the thing to do, it was just one Saturday after all. But of course it wasn't just one Saturday, it was a series of *choices*.

I have no problem with the person who chooses to

dedicate his or her life to being successful in the office or people who consciously eschew personal, family and community life in order to be the world's best at work. But I do when those people expect to also have a healthy balanced life, with family love and affection and a grounded sense of self and community. These people choose to get married, to have children, to live in a community, but then opt to ignore these parts of their lives. When the inevitable train smash arises in their personal lives, they act surprised and confused, as if circumstances had overtaken them and they are victims of mysterious relationship forces that they couldn't possibly hope to understand. More often than not, their isolation is made worse because they have no one to console them – no family and no friends. But of course, this is the trade-off they made, the course they chose. They just weren't thinking about it at the time.

My message is that you *can* have it all in life. You can have a dynamic and interesting professional life. You can have a supportive and loving family. You can maintain your friendships and build up relationships in your local community and areas of interest. But you have to be aware that that is what you want, and *make the choices that will lead you there*.

Choice is around us every day at every moment. I see it when I take my children to the swimming pool. I see other fathers there that *have* taken the decision to be with their kids yet choose to scream down the phone to their office or catch up on some paperwork while they are there. One guy in particular has amazed me for years. Each weekend he turns up with his son for swimming lessons and then he spends the whole lesson on the mobile working on some new deal. Meanwhile his child is having an amazing experience he can't share with his father because mentally he's not even in the pool area. Fathers of this sort have taken the choice to be there, but they haven't really chosen to *be* there. They are not aware of the decisions they are making, or worse, they lie to themselves and their families about the reasons for their decisions.

THE POWER OF DELUSION

Tom is a very successful, charismatic executive. He has built a new business in Australia to the point where it is regarded as a leader in its field. Unfortunately, during this time his marriage broke down.

His children and wife have not coped well with the resultant separation and there continue to be issues in the relationships between the executive and his family. Unexpectedly Tom was offered a role to establish a new business in London. This would provide him with the opportunity to create a global company (based on the model in Australia) and would allow him to really see through his vision for the business. Yet leaving Australia would mean severely limiting the time he could spend with his children, because they would remain with their mother in Australia.

I expected this decision to be a difficult one for him. Surely anyone who was aware of the consequences of abandoning their children would think twice about it. I expected Tom to at least be careful in his considerations. As it happens, he elected to go to London almost immediately. He told himself that his children would benefit from the move.

As he saw it, with him in London, he would see them for a focused period of time every few months – school holidays – and he could take them to wonderful locations around the world. The fact that young children don't really think in terms of exotic holiday destinations never occurred to him. Neither did the fact that children need constant and frequent access to their parents.

I have no problem with Tom's career-related decision. That he wished to go to London to start up a business is fine. But, as I saw it, Tom was creating an elaborate family-related justification for taking an essentially career-related decision. He wants to have it all – successful work life and a good home life. But he does not behave that way. Rather than be honest and say he was putting his career goals ahead of the needs of his children, he constructed this 'reality distortion field' to convince himself he wasn't abandoning his kids, and justify his actions to the children. The kids, who are told that they should be really pleased about the disappearance of their father (when in fact they are very upset), will no doubt be adversely affected.

It is too predictable, and too tragic. Crunchtime is only a matter of years away, but with pots of money and global adulation begging, Tom is simply not thinking about the impact on his children in the future. He is lying to himself, and to his kids.

What a father like Tom has done is to separate within his own psyche the lives of his family from his own life – as if they were actually two separate things. The truth of the matter is that once we embark on the adventure that is having a family, our lives are intimately intertwined, forever. My daughters will always be my daughters, no matter what they do, no matter what I do. How they behave, what they believe, and how they live their lives will always be an important part of my life too, whether I like it or not. Much, much more so than the successes and failures of the companies I work for.

My employees will not be the people who will be by my side when I am old and ill, but I hope my wife will. My work colleagues do not make Christmas and holidays special for me, but my kids do. Similarly, I can't call my clients when I am feeling depressed and need someone to talk to, but I can call my friends. The problem with Tom's artificial separation of family and work lives is that it is based on an unbelievable short-termism. Having entered into a partnership with his wife to have and raise two children, he has let his side of the bargain down, and the decision will inevitably come back to haunt him.

LOOKING EVERYWHERE BUT WHERE IT MATTERS

Charlie is the CEO of a large US organisation. He is regarded as a global leader with many years of out-standing financial performance. Judging by what one reads in the business press, he is the epitome of the twenty-first century business leader, weighed down with accolades and awards, a string of business achievements lying in his wake.

Charlie's personal life doesn't reflect so well on him, however. A couple of years ago his eldest son became involved with drugs. Initially it was the occasional party drug but over time the problem grew. Charlie knew of the situation all along put it down to youthful exuberance.

As his son slipped further into trouble, getting caught stealing money from his parents and his siblings, the executive tried to get the best help for his son. Psychologists, counsellors, mentors, you name it. Any parent would do the same. The problem with Charlie's approach was that he was doing it all remotely – he travelled extensively and even when at home, he worked very long days and had many business functions during the week. His approach to the problem, in other words, was along the lines of 'Which cheque do I sign?'

Before his son had started using drugs, Charlie's wife had pleaded with him to spend more time at home, especially when the son seemed to be developing worrying behaviour. Charlie's response was to try to outsource the problem by bringing in more experts. The experts did help, but you have to wonder why Charlie didn't see the value in taking time out of his schedule. Wouldn't he have wanted to actually be there with his son, talk to him and work alongside the experts?

As I write this, Charlie's son is still having massive problems, and Charlie blames it all on the kid: 'After all, he has had the best schools, money to do what ever he wants, lots of freedom . . .'

What more could a child want?

THE ROLE OF CORPORATE CULTURE

The corporate culture which dictates that people dedicate all their waking hours to work is a self-fulfilling one: targets are set high, and the impression is that the harder you work, the more likely it is that you will hit or exceed them. Senior managers have dedicated themselves to their work and made sacrifices, and they expect the same of their people.

To use the words of Professor Charles Handy of the London Business School: 'If the brightest and best among us have no time for anything or anyone but themselves and their work ... it is the organisation, the customers or the clients who suffer.'

Young people are bred into this culture, in which pulling an all-nighter is considered a badge of honour rather than a sign of management incompetence and indecision. Rather than analyse why an all-nighter was necessary, managers often go home feeling good that they were able to exploit their people and squeeze the lifeblood out of their most valuable resource.

HONEYMOON ON HOLD

A colleague of mine works for a blue-chip investment banking firm. The firm was pitching for a major piece of business from a significant industrial client. Chris, one of the senior members of the team working on the proposal, had planned his wedding some twelve months earlier, my colleague told me, and had booked his honeymoon in France. The pitch for the business was planned for just after he returned from his honeymoon, and everything was prepared and ready.

Two days into the honeymoon, the client called Chris's CEO and asked to change the date of the meeting. This is the kind of request that investment banks don't say no to, although it is unclear whether explaining Chris's situation to the client would have been out of the question.

Instead, the CEO called Chris in France and asked him to come back for the pitch. This he did: he jumped on a plane, came home to deliver the presentation, and the bank won the business. Champagne all around, except, of course, for Chris and his bride whose honeymoon together had been destroyed.

The CEO subsequently used Chris's story as an example of the level of dedication demanded by the bank. My colleague saw Chris's story as an example of at least two people who had completely lost perspective on what exactly was the right level of commitment to a job.

What gets me is the false sense of urgency that is applied to everything a company does. Don't get me wrong, some things *are* urgent and do demand attention – hey, I've lived through Microsoft product-shipping death marches, remember. Some things need to be done and done now, no matter how long it takes. But many things don't. In seminars with clients, I regularly hear how their teams have just pulled all-nighters to get this presentation or that presentation together. What is striking is how often we find out, after a bit of probing, that the all-nighter had been unnecessary.

'The meeting with the client was at 10 in the morning, and it took us all that time to get the presentation right.' Really, it took 27 hours? 'Yes. Every minute.' What if the meeting had been at 11 in the morning? My guess is that it would have taken 28 hours – every minute. If it took right up until the moment of the meeting to get the presentation together, why didn't they call the client and postpone the presentation? Because postponing the meeting wouldn't in fact provide the team with time to rest and recuperate, instead, it would give management an excuse to continue to engineer the presentation to the 2 per cent.

In my experience, a lot of corporate life is engineered to the 2 per cent. What does this mean? It means that a piece of work, a presentation or a report, will be treated like it was a rocket ship going to the moon. It's that important. Any tiny fault will cause calamity and death, and every part must be engineered to be reliable to the 2 per cent. Mostly, though, what we're talking about is a piece of work, a presentation or a report, and not space travel. It is a false sense of importance, of urgency, and it destroys lives.

Decisions like this are taken because companies set the value of their people's lives outside the company at nought. They are 'human resources' from which the greatest return needs to be wrung. I have found that rather than plan the corporate life in such a way as to maximise the productiveness of their people's time in the office, corporate managers actively plan work to use up their people's time. Companies fail to think of their people as people, as if the employment contract gives them a claim on employees' entire lives.

PUT UP WITH IT

Paul, a close friend of mine, is a committed, dedicated performer. A senior executive in one of Australia's most admired top 50 companies, he works a minimum 60-hour week, is constantly flown around the country to attend to crises in the organisation, and has recently, single-handedly, turned a project around from an estimated $50 million loss to a $30 million profit. He is an extremely valuable employee.

Unfortunately, Paul spent just a little too much of his earlier years in rugby mauls, and has recently been diagnosed with a chronic deterioration of parts of his spine. Paul was in a lot of pain, and, crucially, his spine was degrading and he needed surgery to stop it.

He informed his employer of his condition and that he would need to take ten days off when the operation was scheduled, four months away. The response from his boss was that an operation at this time would cause some issues with a major project; he was unhappy but accepted the decision.

Four months later, with the operation taking place in just one week's time, Paul spent three-and-a-half hours with his boss in a meeting. At the end of the meeting, the boss turned to Paul and said, 'You seem to be moving around okay and not in too much pain, so how about you reschedule the operation six months out so that we can minimise the impact on the project?'

Paul was upset but, he explains to me, this is actually completely in concert with the company's general approach. The company comes first and last, and things like employees' families, health and friends should not impact on the company's operation.

The result is that Paul, an outstanding employee, will probably look for employment in another organisation, and this heartless company will lose another talented person. Not all employees in that company can make the switch, however. Many people are being forced to hide their family needs and other issues, to the detriment of their lives, so as to ensure they do not incur the wrath of the workaholic/obsessive CEO.

Organisations like those mentioned above are crazy, driving their people into the ground for the sake of their senior executives' ego and power. Many bosses will say that they are doing it for the sake of the organisation, for its competitiveness.

Charles Handy, a professor at the London Business School who laments the insane trend towards over-dedication in the workplace, writes of the chairman of a large pharmaceutical company who had summed up his employment policy very neatly: $\frac{1}{2} \times 2 \times 3 = P$. Half as many people in his business in five years time, paid twice as much and producing three times as much equals productivity and profit. But it should be the other way around: $2 \times 1 \times 3 \times \frac{1}{2} = P$. Or: twice as many people being paid the same as they now are producing three times as much in half the time. As we saw in the previous chapter, the younger generation is hungry for a life, not just for more money. But companies don't seem to realise this – and I think it will be at their peril, as talented people refuse to give up their lives for the corporate cause.

PART TIME?

After a great deal of pushing and hassle, a well-known legal firm finally agreed to allow female associates to come back to the company part time after they'd had a baby. The associates were happy to receive 50 per cent of their salary for half of the workload – that is what they wanted. Instead, the firm offers them 60 per cent of their former pay. Generous, you'd think. But, according to two people who told me their stories, the workload is structured as follows: they work 9 to 3, four days a week, at the office; they then have to work at home from 7 pm to midnight each night plus most of the fifth weekday to finish the work.

What has clearly happened is that the true workload has remained constant, but they are being paid only 60 per cent for it. More than that, the firm now boasts that it has part-time workers – how diverse and flexible! But, for my friends, billable hours remain the same: they have to have six-and-a-half billable hours each day. How on earth does that stack up as part time? Fine for a partner, perhaps, but not an associate . . .

THE INDIVIDUAL'S RESPONSIBILITY

Of course, people are responsible for their own lives. They do make their own choices, to work for a particular company, for instance, to take on certain responsibilities. The problem is that companies have tools available to them – salaries, power structures, peer group pressure and the like – that can be used to influence their people's choices. So, even when people fully intend to bring balance to their work, to have time for their families and outside interests, companies are in a position to influence people against their resolve. Money distorts our sense of values, and can do real damage to the way we live our lives. In some cases, it can be a treadmill to oblivion.

Another law firm I know uses people's own greed against them. From the company's point of view, it is a wonderful trick, for while it causes great damage, all the victims are desperate for more pain and the company makes even more money.

This company has a policy of paying the highest average salaries in its industry. By higher I mean *significantly* higher. What this initially creates is a bunch of people that can't believe their luck. They are doing the same job as some of their peers from university but are earning (at any level) 30 to 70 per cent more than their peers.

To make this money, the employees have the highest utilisation rates in their service industry and they also have the highest requirement for billable hours per day. So the model seems clear: work harder than others and earn more. Simple and fair.

Of course, working 60 hours a week (minimum) for fifteen-plus years in this organisation does not allow for much of a life outside of work. One would hope that these incredibly smart employees would work out a model where they slotted away the increased income for a certain number of years so that, when they felt like it, they could downshift or modify their work environment. But this is generally not the case.

What they seem to do is say, 'Hey, I now have $3000 more a month, so let's upgrade the house/car/boat etc.' They ratchet up their lifestyle to their new income level (and often to the income level that they can see coming in a couple of years). The problem is, when is enough enough? Rather than stopping at the sufficient, well-decorated apartment conveniently located towards the centre of town, we suddenly need a holiday house – or two holiday houses – and an investment property, a boat, a couple of cars. All of this for a person who works six days a week and much of Sunday as well. All of this so we can say: 'Look at me, I am a success! And I can *prove* it . . .'

But here is the sting. Even if they get tired of the 60-hour weeks, it's impossible for them to take the same job at a rival firm. The working hours would be less demanding, yes, but the subsequent reduction in income of somewhere between 25 and 40 per cent would make it impossible to maintain their lifestyle. They are trapped. The only release is to realise that the trappings of wealth do not in fact define the character of a person. It's an old message but one that is so often missed by apparently intelligent people.

Management guru Lawrence Peter famously wrote that in a hierarchically structured administration, people tend to be promoted up to their 'level of incompetence'. This is the well-known Peter Principle. Applying this to people's lives as a whole, perhaps we could say: *In a haphazardly structured career we take on roles that pay a lot more than we can earn elsewhere, and rather than put this away we increase our lifestyle to map our income level.* I like to think of this as the Petre principle.

CAN YOU BUY HAPPINESS?

Try telling someone struggling to meet mortgage payments that money can't buy happiness. They will, quite rightly, tell you that if only they could have more financial security they would be okay. At one level, this is true, but it is interesting to see what happens at the other end of the spectrum.

A very wealthy Australian businessman I know has made a life out of making money from every deal he gets involved with. As a result, throughout his life he has been surrounded by sycophantic people from investment banking firms, legal firms, charities and the rest, all after a cut of the action. He never seemed to question the motives of his 'friends' and was able to do whatever he wanted by always keeping the interest of the pack in mind.

Very recently though, he lost a great deal of money in two deals that have severely undermined his net wealth. As a result, his entourage has evaporated and he now finds that he doesn't really have any friends. He is an incredibly lonely man, very depressed and very dark on life and what it offers. All this from a guy who is still worth around $40 million. He has his health, he lives a fabulous lifestyle, and with that kind of wealth his opportunities are almost unlimited for whatever he might wish to do. Still, he can't seem to see that he is incredibly lucky. Rather he just sees that he has lost the ability to command a stage and do whatever he wants to the applause of his court of jesters.

The rich are a strange breed. Every year *BRW* magazine publishes a list of Australia's richest people, and every year, many people I know spend sleepless nights worrying about whether they are higher or lower in the list than last year. You really have to wonder what is going on in their minds if they have nothing better to worry about than whether they are worth $300 million or $320 million, or whether they are number 20 in the list or number 25. What sort of values do these people have?

It is a simple message. Success is built of more than what you achieve in the office. The question is, what *is* it built of? That is what we shall look at in the next chapter, 'The meaning of success'.

GENDER IMBALANCE

So you want proof that something is not quite right in terms of gender balance?

I believe that the majority of organisations are run on the basis of a flimsy response to the issue of work–family balance. Within this bias against people having a balanced life is a further bias against women. Specifically, organisations show a general lack of concern for the balance needed by employees as displayed by their requirements for hours worked and interruption of family time. This impacts on all employees but is biased particularly against women.

If you look at most professional services organisations you will see that usually more than half of the graduates coming into the firm are female. This pattern continues through the first few layers of the organisation.

So what happens at partner level or the preceding level? Surely one would expect in this day and age in a profession where the actual work is gender neutral (ie not lifting of heavy objects or some other gender-biased role) that you would expect perhaps half of the partners to be women?

The actual case is that between only five and ten per cent of the partner base in most firms is made up of female employees. Obviously, female graduates are not less skilled than their male counterparts, nor less able to meet the skill requirements of the more senior roles in the firm. The most likely reason is that firms are unable to cope with many female employees' desire to take some time out of work to have their children before returning to the work force, and the desire of female (and sometimes male) employees to return in some part-time capacity.

One of the great cons is the concept that these professional services organisations can't sustain part-time professional roles. Surely, with an appropriate client load, accessibility via the internet, mobile phones and a pro-rata remuneration package, many women would be able to stay in their profession and maintain their partner status.

When I asked one senior partner of a legal firm why 55 per cent of their associates were women and only 5 per cent of them partners, he commented that women wanted to 'go and have babies and then work part-time'. He went on to say that there was no way part-time roles could work in their profession. I asked whether they had actually tried any such schemes, and his response was most enlightening: 'If we did offer part-time partnerships a lot of the men would want to take up the option and that would destroy the firm.' Really? If great minds are applied to the model, surely there would be a way to make this system work for the clients, the employees and the firm as a whole. The question is who cares. The employees care, but it seems the leaders do not.

The reality is the leaders of many of these firms believe that they have paid the price (ie traded their life) for the firm and that anyone who wants to be a leader in the firm needs to make the same trade-off.

THE GLASS CEILING

Mary was a leading partner in a tax firm. She was regarded as one of the top people in her area of expertise in the Melbourne market. She decided to have a baby and took a year off work before returning to work part-time when the baby was one year old. While she was being paid on a part-time basis, her revenue budget was the same as a full-time partner. At this time it was made clear to her that the firm was reluctantly agreeing to the part-time approach due to her years of service.

After a year she found the pressure to be overwhelming and went back full-time. The CEO reacted very positively to this, commenting that he appreciated her 'increased commitment to the firm'.

When her child was three years old she decided to have another baby. When she told the CEO he said there was no way she would be able to return to part-time work.

When the second baby was three months old Mary returned to a full-time role in the firm. Over the next year she worked diligently and delivered exceptional results. Mary was, at this time, very highly regarded by her clients and was meeting all the revenue/profit targets. She was also desperately missing time with her baby. She approached the CEO to ask if she could return to part-time work. The request was refused and Mary subsequently left the firm to work part-time in a smaller practice. The good news is that Mary has now found a good balance between her career and family aspirations. The bad news is that she had to leave a 'big end of town' firm and go to a smaller one to achieve this balance.

TRANSFORMATION

About ten years ago I met an incredibly smart and talented sales executive who worked for a major Australian company in the finance sector. She had all the skills to take her to very senior roles, but she also had a warmth rarely found in senior executives.

A year ago I met her again and was not surprised to find out that she was now a divisional CEO running a large part of a global firm. She was still very confident, smart and focused, but she seemed to have lost the warmth she had exuded years before and had become much more aggressive in her manner. She had become a bloke!

We chatted for a while and I told her that I felt she seemed to have become more aggressive. She explained that early on she had learned that if she wanted to be a success in her male-dominated industry, she had to out macho the men. While this was probably not going to further the cause of women's rights she felt she was being pragmatic.

My experience is that women who have been able to maintain their inherent femininity as well as their job skills make far better CEOs than their aggressive male counterparts – the problem is how to help women move into senior roles without casting off their feminine qualities.

04

THE MEANING
OF SUCCESS

What do we mean when we say someone is 'successful'? As the dictionary has it, we usually mean that they are accomplished in their job, that they have become rich or achieved social recognition and status. Our society is focused on 'success', we put those who have achieved it – or the definition of it – up on a pedestal. We photograph them and put them in the newspaper, write biographies of them, and put them on television. They are our role models.

We are obsessed with success and how to achieve it, however one defines it. Amazon.com returns 124 243 results when you search for books related to the word 'success'. According to Reuters/Dow Jones, 48 100 articles containing the word 'success' in their titles were published in the English-speaking press across the globe during 2003. The articles related to everything from success in zoos and schools through to success rates for complex surgical procedures, 'get rich quick' schemes and how to achieve lasting success in life.

What struck me when browsing the list was that people seem to be able to agree about the meaning of success if they relate it to one particular aspect of life, or one particular measure. For a company, it's the level of annual profit. For a critical medical procedure, it's how many lives it saves. For a house sale, it's either the selling price or the purchase price. For people, it seems it is often money.

TRADE-OFFS FOR SUCCESS

Life is never as simple as it seems, and neither is the concept of success. A recent article by Amanda Ripley in *Time* magazine examined the impact of a US federal government law called 'No Child Left Behind' (NCLB), which stipulates that kids as young as nine meet benchmarks in reading and maths or jeopardise their schools' reputation. The tests affect how much money the school gets from the state, how many of its decisions it can make, and whether or not it stays open. The story tells of Garfield/Franklin elementary school in Ohio, placed on the Schools in Need of Improvement list under the terms of the legislation.

The school underwent a corporate-style rationalisation program with one aim: to get the children over the government's testing hurdles. Reading, in particular, became a focused science. Teachers started reading much more non-fiction to the children, because that is the focus of the tests, students began using computerised reading programs, and test strategies were taught to eight-year-olds. Teachers asked kids as young as seven to sign forms accepting the responsibility to raise their test marks. The school's test marks improved out of sight. That was the good news.

The article focused on the cost to the children and the school community of the single-minded focus on test results. It began with a list of some of the things that the school children could no longer do as a result of the new program: 'eagle watch on the Mississippi River, go on field trips to the University of Iowa's Natural History, and have two daily recesses'. One fifth grade teacher expressed his reservations with the new regimen, which focuses almost exclusively on reading and arithmetic: 'There are parts of NCLB that are positive and good, but there's a huge portion that is horrible. They're not learning civics, history, geography – a lot of essential skills they're going to need.' Other casualties of the new regimen include social studies, creative writing and teacher autonomy.

The story of Garfield/Franklin is a strong metaphor for the way in which we view success in the modern world. The school is training its students to succeed in what is measured – the test results in reading and mathematics – at the expense of some things that arguably *matter* more. The school has recognised that success is a matter of trade-offs, and that it is able to trade its kids' broad-based education for success in a narrow set of metrics.

We do this in our own lives. How often do we read

in the financial press that so-and-so is a huge success because the profits at his company grew strongly? We do not hear whether he dealt fairly with suppliers, whether he was supportive of his employees, whether the culture he developed impacted negatively on the lives of his employees, and whether his company's products or services damaged the environment or the communities in which they operated. The press measures success by the narrowest of metrics, and bestows glory on people for the narrowest of achievements.

Such people have usually worked very hard to achieve success in their chosen field, to amass large fortunes, to build big business empires, to make their mark on society. The rewards of success are often well earned. But my own experience in talking with many 'successful' businessmen is that, while dictionary-defined success provides a certain kind of satisfaction, often it has been achieved at an immense cost. Many have traded their life's most valuable relationships, their interests and in the end themselves for money and power.

This type of trade-off has been discussed in previous chapters – maybe they were simply doing what they felt was expected of them, or maybe, in the whirlwind of career excitement, they never stopped to take stock and consider what their success was costing them in terms of their humanity. But more troubling perhaps is that these executives rarely think about the collateral damage their drive for success has caused to people lower down the food chain in their organisations.

As stated earlier, self-awareness does not come naturally to many CEOs. For them, perhaps the failure to live a full life is compensated by the wheelbarrows full of cash they take home. But what about the middle manager three levels down who has a decent salary but who has been forced, by the CEO, to give up his or her life for the sake of the company?

IT DOESN'T FEEL AS GOOD AS IT SHOULD

I have tested the statement 'It doesn't feel as good as it should' with many successful executives, including CEOs of some of the country's largest and most impressive organisations. There appears to be general agreement: they thought that having all the trappings of supposed success would bring happiness and bliss, yet here they are, feeling empty.

It seems that many outwardly successful people are not in fact happy and fulfilled. Often, if they aren't already divorced, they have poor relationships with their spouses and children, and no friends outside work. They can't bear being away from the office and the symbols of their importance, have no hobbies and are generally dissatisfied with the lives they have built for themselves. And these are the people who outwardly have it all – they are rich, famous and powerful.

The media often tells them that they are a success and with this mantle comes accolades and adulation. Yet they know that their success is very narrowly defined, and in their dark moments they realise how false it all is.

I've asked many of these people whether they might not be happier if they were to let go, but they're hooked: hooked on the drug of money and power. Most feel that if they were to let their facade drop they would be even less happy. The *trappings* of success, one might say.

THE TOMBSTONE TEST

I have written a lot about my own wake-up call when my sister Gabriela died, and how fortunate I was to have answered it. The futility of chasing dictionary-style success for its own sake was brought home to me in Seattle when I was called by my brother-in-law, who was preparing for my sister's funeral. He wanted to know what I thought we ought to put on her tombstone.

For me, the thought of encapsulating one's life in a few short lines was quite profound. It makes you focus on exactly what your life has been about and why. My brother-in-law decided on some lines that expressed what a great loss the world had suffered as a result of Gabriela's death. They were poignant and appropriate, and, as these things should, got me thinking about how I might be described after my death. 'Vice-president, Microsoft Corporation' was all I could come up with.

This would have been nothing to be ashamed of – it was one of my life's great honours. But as I thought about it in the dark days after my sister's death, somehow it was not enough. I wanted my tombstone to read:

> *Successful businessman*
> *Loving husband*
> *Great father*
> *Lifelong friend*
> *Energetic contributor to the community*

The relevance is that many people, including many thriving executives, are so caught up in the day-to-day that they fail to consider what their life is about, or what they would be happy to have written on their tombstones. The day-to-day turns into the year-to-year, which turns into the decade-to-decade. They wake up, aware now that they're trapped in a false image of success, their real lives – family, friends, interests – long gone.

AN UNPOPULATED FUNERAL

In *Heart of Success*, Rob Parsons writes of a young boy, searching for the meaning of success in his business school library. In striking up a friendship with what he thought was the library's janitor, he speaks of his father:

My dad had fifteen thousand employees, twelve board members and no real friends . . . We had a party for his sixtieth birthday, 500 people came. At his funeral there were 50.

Personally, I don't think the number of people likely to attend your funeral is a particularly useful gauge of how successful your life has been. But one of Parsons' points is that, as busy business executives, we tend to feel that we are surrounded by our real lives, when in fact we are surrounded by the paraphernalia of our businesses.

I am not advocating a world filled with people who no longer strive for achievement in their job but one in which people know what they are truly striving for and are sure it is something that really matters to them.

THE MEASUREMENT OBSESSION

To live a truly successful life, it is clear that we need to move away from the idea of measuring success using simple parameters like how much money you have or the market capitalisation of the company you will be running for the next 2.9 years. The problem is that in our society we are obsessed with these measurements, and if it can't be measured, it doesn't exist – like social studies at Garfield/Franklin elementary school. School exams are just the first example – children are cut out of their futures, and schools are denied funds because of the marks they achieve in particular exams. I couldn't become a doctor because I froze up on the day of my industrial arts exam, even though I knew the subject backwards. It is harsh, and maybe necessary, but who could argue that it is a holistic way of measuring my fitness for medicine or the best possible way of organising people's futures?

In medicine itself, some organisations measure the success of their treatments by the number of years they put on patients' lives, without considering the impact of those treatments on the quality of patients' lives. In *Quality of Life: The Missing Measurement in Healthcare*, Lesley Fallowfield, a psychologist, writes about the last few weeks of a friend's life. The friend, aged in her early thirties, was critically ill with leukaemia, and both chemo and radiation therapy had been unsuccessful. The side effects of the therapy had made her friend more ill than the illness itself, and had condemned her to spend the last days of her life inside a sterile plastic bubble with no physical contact with family or friends. 'I am still haunted by the last conversation we had,' Fallowfield remembers, 'when she asked why I had not tried to dissuade her from a therapy with poor chances of survival, but a high chance of destroying the quality of whatever life she had left.'

When we measure our successes by simple yard-sticks it distorts the way we behave. When waiting lists are used to gauge a hospital's success, for instance, suddenly a lot of cataracts and trick knees are fixed, leaving more serious illnesses to wait in the corridors. And anybody that has a passing familiarity with the way corporate budgets are produced knows the powerful impact they have on people's behaviour. Quirky things happen as a result: huge boosts in spending from the marketing department in May and June as the financial year comes to a close, amazing lowballing of bonus-related sales targets, which are miraculously smashed year after year, or the outrageous politics that go on during budget-setting season. And yet these numbers, a sub-genre of science fiction really, are how we determine the success or not of our company, or our department, or our sales team.

Look at the swathe of company scandals that washed across the front pages a few years back: Enron, Tyco and WorldCom in the USA, HIH in Australia, Parmalat and Ahold in Europe, SK Global in Korea. All of these were a result of the business world's propensity to measure success by a simple yardstick – whether that be EPS, net profits, or market share – and so motivate managers to distort the working of their companies and boost that figure at the expense of almost everything else. Many of the leaders of these companies, once the masters of their universes, are now financially and emotionally destroyed, in jail or on their way there. At the time, these CEOs were held up as great suc-cesses, and yet all we knew was that their organisation had achieved (for a very brief time!) an impressive EPS.

The measurement disease has spread throughout society. Economists are obsessed with GDP growth figures, and yet, as we shall see in the next chapter, economic growth does not make us happier. GDP, like your annual salary, is too simplistic a measure to capture all the things that we need in our lives to consider them a success. In the 1960s, the late Robert Kennedy was famous for his views on the similarly inadequate GNP, America's economic equivalent.

> *The GNP measures neither wit nor our courage, neither our wisdom nor our learning, neither our compassion nor our devotion to country. It measures everything, in short, except that which makes life worthwhile.*

Anybody who knows how national statistics are put together will understand that GNP or GDP, as a number, is as much a fantasy as corporate accounts. But we cling to it because it is a simple measure, and we need to feel like we have progressed, that we are *growing*.

The economy is in the best shape it has ever been, we are told. According to the business section of *The Australian* on 6 March 2004, 'The bubbly is flowing freely in the champagne Australian economy.' Yet at the same time we are seeing increased levels of child poverty, a dramatic increase in antidepressant prescriptions, and people are working longer hours and sacrificing more of their lives. How can this be? We are simply measuring the wrong data.

MEASURING THE DAMAGE

What is most worrying is that our tendency to measure everything using simple numbers has a real impact on people's lives. In my own work, one measurement I am concerned with is the following equation:

Effectiveness at work = number of hours spent on the job

It is such a simple equation and so blatantly false that it's hard to take seriously, and yet the average white-collar executive uses it as the basis for a working life. People with this mindset often have another measure they use when dealing with people at work:

Success = power over others

Power over others = a licence to abuse them

In many large corporations the exercise of power is explicit and brutal. One large Australian company I know grades its people by numbers, with senior management being level one, all the way down to the ungraded untouchables. The chief executive of this company will not speak to anyone that's level four or below, as a matter of *policy*. Not because he doesn't come into contact with them or because he has nothing to say to them and vice versa, but simply because to do so would violate the personal principles of power that he has set up for himself.

Then there's the subject of manners. Most people, when offered a cup of coffee at a party or in a restaurant, would at least say thank you. Not in the corporate boardroom. Usually the only response is a surly bark ('Latte!'), delivered without even looking at the admin staff or waiter.

What gives people the right to behave in this way? Could they get away with it at home? Imagine this same executive being asked by his wife if he wants a coffee, placing his drink order without even turning away from the footy on TV to look at her. The reason they behave in this rude manner in the corporate environment is because they can. For the most part, the low-salaried admin person knows that to tell the boss he's being rude will mean a fast ride out the door. So the office minions and waiters take the abuse, and who knows, maybe his wife does also.

This is just a small example of power gone mad. Power without any checks and balances. While it may start with a lack of common courtesy and basic manners, this same abuse of power sees the likes of Jack Welch retiring as GE's chief executive with hundreds of millions of dollars yet being given unlimited use of the company jet. Can you imagine a former bus driver demanding access to the company bus fleet in his retirement? To quote Abraham Maslow: 'The person who seeks power is . . . likely to be the one who shouldn't have it. Such people are apt to . . . use it for their own selfish gratifications.'

In the 'Corporate culture' chapter, we will see how these equations impact on the work environment and how they are a direct cause of many organisations' problems. At the root of this issue is a false separation we have between work and our lives, as if we take off our real selves when we walk into the office and hang them on the coat rack. Many executives can only live with themselves by believing that what they do in the office is not who they really are. The irony is that those that are best able to separate themselves from their actions are the ones most likely to work the longest hours, and so end up losing themselves in the process.

THE SYNERGISTIC BLACKFOOT

In our society, we measure success using a few overly simplistic yardsticks: money, power, toys. But not everyone is like this. Other societies offer alternative models.

Abraham Maslow was a pioneer of management psychology. He came up with the term 'self-actualisation' (what we are all striving for), and developed his hierarchy of needs – food, water and shelter being at the bottom, love and esteem in the middle, and self-actualisation at the top. In 1938, Maslow undertook some anthropological research among the Blackfoot Indian tribes of Canada and found that their idea of success was very different from the American concept.

The first virtue of the tribe was generosity. The most successful people in the tribe therefore were the most generous. Maslow described the Sun Dance ceremony in which all the people who had accumulated possessions over the course of the year would give them away until they were left with only the clothes they were standing in. Their reward? True prestige was won by those who parted with as much as they could give, while hoarding assets or knowledge was reviled.

The needs of the tribe as a whole were not set up in competition with the needs of the individuals, but each reinforced the other. Instead of a general leader with general power, the tribe had different leaders for different situations. The leader of the Sun Dance, for instance, was not expected to be the one who negotiated with the government. Each leader was chosen for a particular job based on the needs of that job.

Through extensive testing, Maslow discovered that the Blackfoot suffered from less self-doubt and self-consciousness than people from more competitive cultures and ways of life. It was as if each tribe member knew his strengths and weaknesses. Weaknesses were not ostracised but accepted as a normal part of the human condition.

Is it a coincidence that much modern literature on the art of management talks about the necessity for leaders to know themselves, to understand their weaknesses, and to use this knowledge to establish their position and respect within their organisations?

ALTERNATIVE DEFINITIONS OF SUCCESS

The story of the Blackfoot Indians clearly shows that the idea of success is culturally determined. There is no innate human trait dictating that ownership of the latest MP3 player is a prerequisite for a successful life. Buddhist monks, who dedicate their lives to exorcising the demons of desire, certainly don't think it a prerequisite for success. Neither do most spiritual leaders – rich men having as much trouble getting into heaven as camels through needle eyes, and all that.

Throughout history, man has grappled with the concept of success, bound up as it is with the meaning of life. For the remainder of this chapter I have collected together some quotes from historical figures on their impressions of the meaning of success, and very revealing they are too. The first is from Albert Einstein:

> *He is considered successful in our day who*
> *gets more out of life than he puts in. But a*
> *man of value will give more than he receives.*

Clearly the man who developed relativity theory and whom *Time* magazine voted the Person of the Twentieth Century was no stranger to success. But Einstein knew a thing or two about human nature as well.

> *Success is not the key to happiness.*
> *Happiness is the key to success. If you love*
> *what you are doing, you will be successful.*

Simple, home truths from Albert Schweitzer, philosopher, humanitarian, medical doctor, missionary and the winner of the 1952 Nobel Peace Prize. Schweitzer spent much of his life in Africa and met successful people from all walks of life.

> *The world is moved along, not only by the*
> *mighty shoves of its heroes, but also by the*
> *aggregate of the tiny pushes of each honest*
> *worker.*

That Helen Keller felt her chief duty was to accomplish humble tasks seems a bit strange given the fact that she was one of the most celebrated heroes of her day. An orphan, who contracted a disease before her second birthday leaving her deaf and blind, Keller went on to become a leading figure in the campaigns on behalf of civil rights, human dignity, women's suffrage and world peace. It seems humility was at the heart of her own path to success.

> *I have learned, that if one advances confidently in the direction of his dreams . . . he will meet with a success unexpected in common hours.*

Literature and writing about success tends to focus on how 'success' can be achieved, rather than on what success actually is. This quote from Henry David Thoreau, one of America's greatest essayists, is an example.

> *To follow without halt, one aim; there is the secret of success. And success? What is it? I do not find it in the applause of the theatre; it lies rather in the satisfaction of accomplishment.*

Another quote from the category, this one from Anna Pavlova, opera diva.

> *What I must do is all that concerns me, not what the people think. This rule, equally*

arduous in actual and intellectual life, may serve for the whole distinction between greatness and meanness. It is the harder, because you will always find those who think they know what is your duty better than you know it. It is easy in the world to live after the world's opinion; it is easy in solitude to live after our own; but the great person is one who in the midst of the crowd keeps with perfect sweetness the independence of solitude.

Ralph Waldo Emerson, like Thoreau, was a transcendentalist, a progressive philosopher who wrote about reintegrating the human spirit with the material world. The quote above relates particularly to the role of the leader.

It is not the critic who counts, not the man who points out how the strong man stumbled, or where the doer of deeds could have done better. The credit belongs to the man who is actually in the arena, whose face is marred by dust and sweat and blood, who strives valiantly, who errs and comes short again and again, who knows the great enthusiasms, the great devotions, and spends himself in a worthy cause, who at best knows achievement and who at the worst if he fails at least fails while daring greatly so that his place shall never be with

those cold and timid souls who know
neither victory nor defeat.

A comment on leading from the front by a man who knew a fair bit on the subject. Theodore Roosevelt, as well as being the twenty-sixth president of the USA, organised the building of the Panama Canal and was recipient of the 1906 Nobel Prize for Peace.

He has achieved success who has worked
well, laughed often, and loved much.

This reference to love from American author Elbert Hubbard is most inspiring. One of the most basic human needs is to feel a connection with another person as the sense of belonging is key to our health and wellbeing. This makes sense at home, where we often apply a great amount of resources and energy into creating a caring and loving environment. But at work, where we spend the majority of our waking hours, it's everyone for themselves.

Success is peace of mind, a direct result
of . . . knowing that you did your best to
become the best that you are capable of
becoming, and not just in a physical way.

What attracts me to these words from John Wooden, basketball player and legendary coach, is the emphasis on more than one measure of success. For Wooden, spirituality matters too.

Success is a journey, not a destination.

Although written by a success guru, Ben Sweet-land, this quote has strong resonance, if only because it is so contrary to what we see and hear every day. Success, we are told by the media, is defined by the meeting of the goal, and it seems there is something decidedly Machiavellian in all of this. It does not seem to matter how we achieved the goal, what matters is that we got there. Surely this makes no sense – are we truly defined by a series of achievements or should we be judged on how we conducted our lives, day in, day out? The former is easy to measure, the latter nearly impossible, and so we settle for what is easy to measure.

Many people tell me that they would be happy and feel successful if only they could get to this role or buy that asset. They miss the fact that the *journey* is what we spend our time on and the goal is merely one destination in the journey of life.

> *You are not here merely to make a living.*
> *You are here in order to enable the world to*
> *live more amply, with greater vision, with*
> *a finer spirit of hope and achievement.*
> *You are here to enrich the world, and*
> *you impoverish yourself if you forget the*
> *errand.*

Inspiring stuff from another former US president, Woodrow Wilson. For leaders in particular, this is a pertinent thought. Those who have the opportunity to lead need to have a keen sense of their role in society, not just in their organisation. The key point here is that as a leader you have a responsibility to those that you lead.

> *To laugh often and much*
> *To win the respect of intelligent people and*
> *the affection of children*
> *To earn the appreciation of honest critics*
> *and to endure the betrayal of false friends*
> *To appreciate beauty*
> *To find the best in others*
> *To leave the world a bit better whether*
> *by a healthy child, a garden patch or a*
> *redeemed social condition*
> *To know even one life has breathed easier*
> *because you have lived*
> *This is to have succeeded.*

My personal favourite of all the definitions of success. This quote is often attributed to Ralph Waldo Emerson, although more recently it has been acknowledged as Emerson's adaptation of the writings of Bessie Stanley. Whatever, I find it quite profound.

Just like a life's worth, success is not easy to measure and nor should it be. We must not allow our lives or our efforts to be defined in the simple models demonstrated by the media. To get a complete picture of the success of a life, we need to take into account not simply that a CEO increased the company's profits by 30 per cent a year for five years, but also that while doing this he divorced his wife, as the case may be, and/or one of his children ended up in rehab.

We should not undervalue the financial contribution made by the CEO but we must also appreciate what he traded for it. We should not elevate the corporate leader to some exalted state on the basis of one calculation, in other words. To do so implies that nothing else matters, and suggests that the executive is someone whose life could serve as a role model.

Everything in life requires a trade-off or compromise. Nothing is free. You can't expect to have extreme achievement in any facet of your life without trading off some level of achievement in another area. Only if we are given the full picture of a person's life can we make a more robust judgement on whether they are truly a success.

05

CORPORATE CULTURE

The idea behind this book is that success as the foundation for a life is a multidimensional concept, and that it ought to be defined primarily by *you*. An important corollary to that is that if you are a business leader, then how you define success for yourself has an immense impact on those around you, your family, your friends and also, importantly, your employees at work.

One of the best ways of illustrating the impact of your personal definition of success on other people's lives is through the culture of your company. Everyone knows that companies have a culture, but, as stated previously, it is not often enough that CEOs will take the time to think about it and act on it. From time to time you will hear a CEO talk about the vision of the organisation but rarely do they try to understand the operating culture and the impact of that culture on the business and the employees. I have spoken to CEOs who say, with great pride, that they have an aggressive or competitive culture, with no regard to whether this is good or what the impact of the culture has been (positive or negative) on their employees.

In his book *The New Leaders*, Daniel Goleman argues that the operating culture of an organisation can have a 50–70 per cent impact on the overall performance of the organisation. Culture matters.

DYSFUNCTIONAL CORPORATE CULTURE

Imagine a company, let's call it XYZ Corp. It is similar to a number of companies I have worked with in recent years. Operating in a recently deregulated and very fast growing industry, XYZ is one of the dominant players in its market. Partly because it lacked any competent competition, it grew enormously over the course of the 1990s, saw great success when establishing itself in new markets, and increased both the number of customers and its turnover.

But in recent years, things have been less gratifying. With the company's growth came a large increase in the levels of management, and bureaucracy; the result is that a good portion of the executives are 'managers' rather than 'leaders', and XYZ's structure has become increasingly irrational and inefficient. A surprisingly large number of these managers – hundreds in fact – are supervising just one individual.

During the years when the company was doing well, the managers attributed this success to themselves, and began to believe that they were simply the best at what they were doing. With this came a real arrogance that even outsiders to the company could sense when they had dealings with XYZ. This arrogance bred some idiosyncratic and quite obnoxious behaviour.

Now internal politicking is the dominant management activity, and politically related issues the principal subject of communication. Managers' prestige is determined by the number of people who report to them, so their overriding preoccupation is how to increase their 'empire'. The cor-porate hierarchy is formal and rigidly adhered to. An employee's ranking determines who they can abuse and who they can be abused by when they go in to the office every day. Intimidation operates from the top of the company to the bottom.

Managers determine how punctual they need to be for meetings by how senior they are, because their time is explicitly more important than anybody else's. Bullying is rampant; absenteeism is rife. When things go wrong – which happens more and more frequently – blame is thrown. Many employees simply cruise their days away, spending time shuttling between the coffee machine, their desks and taking breaks, and actually feel resentful if they have to do some work. Shifting responsibility and workloads takes up a lot of people's time.

When employees get together for drinks after work, the main mode of conversation is a good whinge. Customer relationships are suffering because client-facing people are too focused on what is going on inside the company to be concerned about what customers need.

People within the company don't know how to lead others because they haven't been well led themselves.

Most of all, the company's people are unhappy, because they feel they are being treated like a cog in a machine. When you think about it, the terms 'human resources' and 'human capital' are pretty obnoxious, alienating even. But that is the way a company like XYZ treats its people, as objects, things to be traded, invested in, or divested at will. This is another example of how executives leave their real selves at the door when they come in to the office in the morning.

In the previous chapter we saw how these kinds of issues flow on directly from measuring the wrong things (the two equations); from defining success in a particular way. If managers are accorded prestige by how many people report to them, it is only natural that they strive to build their own fiefdoms within the company, and spend the greatest part of their time politicking to make it happen. XYZ's managers are chronically late for meetings because they do not value other people's time as much as they value their own: their value system is distorted by their own conception of 'success'. Success means promotion, and promotion means they have the right to abuse those who work for them. To repeat Daniel Goleman's estimate, apart from the sheer amount of stress and human misery it creates, the problem with an unhealthy corporate culture is the impact it has on the company's performance. Culture has a 50–70 per cent impact on the performance of an organisation.

It is not difficult to believe this. One day spent in an organisation with an unhealthy culture reveals exactly how unproductive and wasteful time spent at the office can be. Think of all the hours evaporated by dull and pointless meetings, political correspondence, and simple time-wasting. This is all time that could be spent creating success – work success or personal success.

WHAT ARE COMPANY VALUES?

So corporate culture is intimately related to an organisation's 'values' and to its 'mission'. It is no wonder then that so many companies are concerned to have strong values. According to a study by Patrick Lencioni, published in the *Harvard Business Review* in July 2000, 55 per cent of all companies claimed integrity as a core value. Strange, but in my experience, companies that really do have integrity are very much in the minority. In the same study, 49 per cent espoused customer satisfaction as a core value. In truth, satisfied customers are much more the exception than the rule.

Think of Enron, a company that had a rich store of visions and values – marvellous words on the page. Its core values were communication, respect, integrity and excellence. But tracking the recent events involving criminal prosecution of Enron's top executives, one might question whether these values were ever referenced or adhered to in any way.

For a company to truly live by its values, and to benefit from all the good things that flow from doing so, it has to understand them as more than a set of nice words. How often have you gone through a pretentious exercise to determine your company/division/business group's 'mission statement' or 'core values' and then carried on business as usual from 9 am the next day? The whole exercise becomes a waste of time and energy, and yet another source of cynicism. The problem is that it has to be the senior executives that get behind the lofty sentiments. From the CEO down, they have to reform how they themselves behave towards people, towards the aims and objectives of the organisations, and ultimately to how they live their lives. It is extremely difficult work.

If a management team is clever enough to work out what its mission, vision and values are in the first place, it has just taken the first step. Ultimately the question is whether they can take on the behaviours that support those values. In my experience, it is only leaders who have a real sense of balance in their own lives, are self-aware and thus aware of the impact of their behaviour on others that are able to take on the kind of behaviour that a healthy corporate culture needs.

GOOD MANAGEMENT/HEALTHY CULTURE

The traits of a dysfunctional organisation are easy enough to spot, and we have more experience of them then we do of healthy ones. So what would a positive corporate culture look like? Healthy companies display the opposite traits to dysfunctional ones, and, according to all the evidence, simply perform better than dysfunctional ones.

David Maister is an internationally renowned expert on the management of professional services firms. In *Practice What You Preach*, he surveyed 139 offices of 29 firms in 15 countries across 15 lines of business, and asked a simple question: are employee attitudes correlated with financial success? Unsurprisingly, since 'People are our most valuable resource' (as the cliche goes), the answer was yes. More than that, Maister found that employee attitudes were determined, not by what management said, but by what management did.

In Maister's study, the operations that had the best financial performance were the ones that scored higher when their people were asked whether: management listened; management valued input; management was trusted; managers were good coaches; management communication was good; managers practised what they preached; and people treated each other with respect.

What's more, motivating people by simply treating them well is much cheaper than motivating them by paying them more. According to chairman Alan Binder, the 1990 Brookings Institution conference on pay and bottom-line performance concluded that 'changing the way workers are treated may boost productivity more than changing the way they are paid,' with worker participation helping to make plans like profit sharing, gain sharing and employee stock ownership work better.

A similar scenario played out in the UK, where Midland Bank (now HSBC) was spending £6 million on a staff reward scheme. The bank found that what most employees actually wanted was for their manager to say 'Well done' occasionally. It then saved two-thirds of the money from the scheme by teaching managers how to go about it.

In the cut-and-thrust world of business, it might seem incongruous to turn towards the Vatican for a definition of the corporation's role, but Pope John Paul II provides this gem:

The purpose of a business firm is not simply to make a profit, but is to be found in its very existence as a community of persons who in various ways are endeavouring to satisfy their basic needs and who form a particular group at the service of the whole society.

It comes back to the fact that employees are people, and people do not want to be treated like a cog in a machine. They have innate needs. According to Abraham Maslow, all people want the following:

- To have self-determination
- To be able to plan and carry out and succeed
- To expect success
- To like responsibility, or at any rate to assume it willingly, especially for themselves
- To be active rather than passive
- To have autonomy
- To have others acknowledge their capabilities fairly.

As managers we all readily acknowledge these wants in ourselves. Why, then, do we have such trouble acknowledging them in our employees?

MAKING THE CHANGE

The question for those executives who find themselves leading a dysfunctional organisation is what to do. Even the simplest of change programs are complex and fraught with risk, let alone ones that are aimed at changing the way hundreds, perhaps thousands, of people behave towards each other. Where on earth to start?

The answer can only be with yourself. Organisational dysfunction exists because its people's definition of success is skewed towards the wrong behaviours, which can only be because senior management's own definition of success is based on a flawed set of values. Somehow, somewhere along the journey to the top job, the corporate leader has allowed himself (or more rarely herself) to start to believe that the measure of their success is the delivery of the annual business plan. This is an easy trap to fall into because we like things we can measure, and measuring the financials is both easy and relevant. Relevant but not sufficient. We need to actively measure the culture we have created and the values that underpin this culture. We need to confront these values and determine whether they truly support a sustainable organisation and a value set we are genuinely proud of.

We need to constantly measure the impact of our behaviour on others. It is only with this insight that any person, CEO or otherwise, can start to unravel the connection between their values and supporting behaviours, and their influence on the organisation's values and supporting behaviours. According to Kotter and Heskett, the most successful change programs happen when top management actively leads away from dysfunction by 'walking the walk'. One or two top managers will provide active leadership by recognising the company's situation and convincing people that crisis is at hand. Through their words and their deeds, they are able to communicate a new vision and a new set of strategies and values for the firm, and they motivate others in the firm to follow their example, and provide vision and values-led leadership.

As a result of the new atmosphere and strategies, the company's performance improves, which in itself creates a new and lasting corporate culture, fundamentally different from the dysfunctional firm of old. This improved performance in effect reinforces the new corporate culture, both in terms of the company's values and the behaviours that match those values, and the new culture continuously improves the company's performance. The vicious circle of arrogance and abuse has been replaced by a virtuous circle of humility and leadership.

To change the behaviour of an entire organisation is a huge challenge. But, as an individual, and as a leader, you can only start with yourself. Starting with yourself is far and away the most effective way of influencing your organisation. Kotter and Heskett found that leadership behaviours have up to 15 per cent influence on the performance of a company. How? Leaders influence their organisations through the corporate culture. Daniel Goleman reckons that leaders have a 20–30 per cent impact on the culture of an organisation, and culture has a 50–70 per cent impact on the performance of the company. By implication then, leaders have a 10–20 per cent impact on the company's performance.

As a leader, *it is up to you* to adopt the behaviour that you would expect to see in your people. And it is only by understanding what you see as success that you will be able to translate that into a set of behaviours that can provide the foundation for a healthy corporate culture.

CHANGE IN PRACTICE

Some time ago, when working on the book *Father and Child*, I spoke with a CEO who was regarded as successful (in monetary terms) but was also seen as abusive, difficult to get on with and someone with a greatly inflated ego. He wanted to address an issue with regard to his working relationship with his senior management team. Apparently it had come to the attention of the board that all was not well between the CEO and his senior team, and they wanted something done about it.

I was brought on as an executive coach for the CEO. Early on it became clear that the use of aggression was the way the CEO felt he should behave and that this behaviour enabled him to avoid revealing any of his weaknesses. Over time we discussed where this conditioning may have come from, and to what extent he really believed in the value of such behaviour. Weeks later we had a breakthrough when the CEO declared that he was willing to try to be truly more open with his staff. Over the period that we had worked together, slowly but surely, the CEO came to see that he had become something he didn't like but he felt trapped by what he had created.

Initially the new behaviour came across as a little bit too contrived, but his staff saw past this. They saw a man desperately trying to change and needing their support.

Years later, I can report that not only does the CEO feel much happier in himself, but relations with his senior team (and their teams) have improved dramatically, leading to improved performance across the group.

The CEO believes that the increased financial performance of his organisation is due, in part, to the new behaviours he is using and the ripple effect of this approach. As pleasing as the financial performance improvements are, I was equally gratified to see someone who could be themselves, treat people as equals and return to the human race.

Where to start?

Let's assume that you have accepted my argument: that a company's values and behaviours are determined by those of top management, and that an unhealthy culture can be changed if top management changes. The question then becomes, where to start?

Clearly, the starting point has to be understanding the kind of behaviours the company needs to develop in order to begin functioning correctly, and identifying the behaviours it needs to discourage in order to move past its dysfunction. The leaders of the company must have an absolutely clear understanding of the role of values in the company's operations, and live and breath them. They have to communicate ceaselessly about vision and values, like a broken record, so that the company's people understand that this is not a fad or a trend, but the underlying principle by which the company will be managed.

Importantly, leaders have to actively discourage dysfunctional behaviours; arrogance, bullying, politicking and disrespect are out – for the leader as well as for the followers. Mutual respect, listening and trust are in.

Changing your behaviour

There is a distinct causal link between your own personal behaviour and the culture within your organisation, and between the business performance of the company and its culture. By consciously determining the kind of behaviours that the company needs in order to produce the results it seeks, and by embodying those behaviours in their own daily lives, leaders can have an active impact on the way that people within their organisations treat each other, the objectives they set for themselves, and the results that they are able to achieve.

People are tribal creatures. We take on and adopt the accepted norms of behaviour that are passed down by our leadership figures. By embodying positive and balanced values, successful business people are able to have an impact much wider than their own circle of influence, as others take on those behaviours in turn and influence others:

1. Top management determines the goals of the business, the strategies it will undertake to achieve those goals, and the supporting behaviours that will be needed in order to achieve them.
2. Top management actively takes on those new behaviours, acting as a converting force, constantly communicating about the business strategy and how people must behave in order to execute it.
3. The message is picked up by others in the company that behaviours and mindsets need to change within the company in order to achieve its goals.
4. People begin to revise the way that they behave when they are at work.

5. The systems and processes of the company are realigned to support the new set of behaviours, motivating staff to change.
6. People are coached and trained to help in the process of change, and are given the skills and the competencies needed to operate in the new environment.
7. They begin to behave in a new way.
8. The new behaviours, combined with new systems and processes, have an impact on people's performance, and the success of their jobs.
9. The company moves towards achieving its strategic goals.
10. Higher levels of performance reinforce the new behaviours, which in turn impact on the success of business outcomes.

It's down to you

Unfortunately, because top management's concept of success is often forged in a negative environment, bad corporate culture is the norm, not the exception. The question is, who is responsible and what can be done? Perhaps controversially, my theory is that an unhealthy corporate culture is the fault of the company's leader, the CEO. It follows, then, that the only person who can do anything about it is also the CEO: if you are that person it is simply down to you.

Many CEOs I have spoken to deny this – it is neither their fault nor their responsibility. The culture lies at the door of the people who live it, they say, or middle management, or the markets, sheer bad luck, poor recruitment policies . . . anything or anyone, it seems, except themselves. Some even suggest that it doesn't even matter. This argument is a cover for the approach that says: 'I am only here for three or four years and in that time I can get the financial performance I need to get my super bonus by using whatever tactics I like.' For what it's worth, as we've seen in this chapter, the world's top business academics disagree.

Too often we see the following cycle in organisations. The new CEO arrives with the support of the board, promising a dramatic turnaround in the organisation's financial performance (thus taking the heat off the board!). They start with a version of 'This is much worse than I imagined', launch a range of cost-cutting measures and urge people to work harder because 'We are in trouble'. After a couple of years they parachute out on a big financial package, leaving behind the rest of the staff at the mercy of another CEO, who starts the cycle again – 'This is much worse than I imagined . . .'

Again: culture does matter. It matters to every person whose life is impacted by the way the organisation behaves and the demands it puts on employees. The leader of the organisation needs to understand the impact of the culture they have created or nurtured and they need to work towards fixing the culture. If you are a CEO, you are the leader of the organisation. You are the only one with the real power to change. But that change must come from you, and it must start with you – your attitudes, behaviours, goals and, ultimately, your definition of success and how that is addressed within your own life.

Nobody said leadership was easy. Having fought their way up the corporate ladder, or forged a successful organisation out of nothing, many leaders feel they have the right to enjoy the fruits of their labours. The question is, how do we define those fruits? If the costs of leadership are high, then surely the privilege of leadership is to have the right to live a successful life: one that takes in all of life's facets. More than that, surely one privilege of leadership is the ability to enable others to live successful and fulfilling lives?

Hopefully the goal of any CEO is that they leave a company (after two, five or ten years) a better and more sustainable organisation than the one they found when they began their tenure. Leaving something positive behind has as much to do with enhancing the lives of those you work with as it does with corporate strategy and execution. A century from now, what house you lived in or car you drove will not matter. The legacy you will leave is the impact on the lives of those you have lived and worked with. It is through their actions as they grow that you will have created a legacy of value. That is the true meaning of leadership.

06

SUSTAINABLE LEADERSHIP

You hear it all the time, but that doesn't make it any less true: leadership in the modern business world is complex and challenging; shareholders demand returns; the business environment is constantly changing; competition is fierce; technology is complex, expensive and an integral part of our lives. And people are as difficult to understand and manage as ever.

Against this background all successful executives want the same things: they want to have a long and financially rewarding career; they want to have the opportunity to make an impact and to be promoted into increasingly responsible positions; they want peer and industry recognition; and after their full-time working career is over they want to continue to be relevant, to have strong relationships and to have an impact. At the same time, everybody wants to maintain strong relationships with their family and friends, keep their health, have the time and energy to explore outside interests, and also to become involved with their communities in some way. In short, we all want to have a balanced and fulfilling life.

Each of these elements is an integral part of the mix that provides an executive with a holistic balance that they can use to maximise their own performance in all parts of life. In my experience, there are three variables that will influence an individual's ability to provide sustainable leadership:

1. The work environment
2. Their own job skills
3. Their personal state.

OBSTACLES TO SUSTAINABLE LEADERSHIP

But there is a fundamental problem. Having had the privilege of working with a number of CEOs in recent years, I have come to understand that the life of the business leader is fundamentally torn between two competing forces.

On the one hand sustainable performance relies on having the appropriate environment, skills and personal state. On the other hand, the environment for chief executives in public organisations is fundamentally unsupportive of a leader who is attempting to be sustainable in both their job and their personal life.

Individuals with the closest match of job skills to those required and who are in the best possible personal state are able to achieve some degree of sustainable leadership over the medium term. Without these attributes, executives are destined for a massive wake-up call in their career and their personal life. But at the same time, all the influences on the executive's life dictate *against* balance.

Many of these influences stem from an illusion of CEO invincibility and omnipotence:

- **Unrealistic board expectations:** In order to ensure their tenure, CEOs have to make big promises, promises that may be met in the short term but will undermine the possibility of sustainability in the medium term.
- **Unrealistic shareholder expectations:** Capital markets are competitive, and investors have a low patience threshold. Shareholders expect consistently increasing value and dividends, and will make the CEO's life miserable if it doesn't happen.
- **Public exposure:** The CEO's life is exposed to the full glare of publicity. Everything from their strategic thinking and forecasts for the next quarter through to their marriage breakdowns and personal foibles are open for inspection.
- **Total responsibility:** Although the company may have tens of thousands of employees, if something goes wrong in even the most obscure part of the company, it is the CEO who is held to account.
- **Change at lightning speed:** With the consistently changing competitive and economic environment, CEOs can go to sleep at night comfortable with their company's strategic position but be locked out of the market by the morning.
- **Regulatory intervention:** Government agencies and regulators are intervening in the affairs of business more than

ever before. CEOs have to be part businessperson, part lobbyist to get anything done these days.

- **Political pressure:** Every organisation has its monsters, pushing and jostling to grab the CEO's ear. Just managing internal ructions would be a full-time job in itself.

With these pressures and more, it is no wonder that business leaders are at risk of losing sight of the bigger picture within their lives. All this is exacerbated by a long-hours culture, and a macho work ethic dictating that work is the unassailable number one priority that drowns out everything else in a 'successful' person's life. Each of these factors means that, for my money, the biggest challenge for the business leader is not in fact to get things right in the workplace – although that is no mean feat – but to create space and time within which they can develop the other two equally important contributors to sustainable leadership: job skills and a decent personal state.

A CRISIS OF LEADERSHIP

The clash between what is necessary for sustainable leadership and the way the world influences us amounts to a crisis of leadership. And the evidence is everywhere. If CEOs were happy in their jobs and were good at them, they would be in them for a long time. But they aren't: the average tenure of a CEO in public organisations in Australia is between 2.5 and four years – just enough time for them to rip the guts out of the organisation and artificially boost the share price so they can get their bonus and head for the border.

When figuring out what your role is as a leader, I find

that it is just as helpful to determine what your role is *not*. By doing this, you can free up large swathes of space and time in which to concentrate on garnering the skills you will need to be sustainably successful, as well as developing a healthy environment that can support and sustain you in your work.

JOB SKILLS

In today's environment, business leaders as much as anyone need to invest in their own competencies. CEOs need the space and time to develop core skills. Many of these skills will have been developed over the course of their careers, but continuous improvement applies to the sustainable leader as much as to the business process. The list of capabilities for the modern business leader is long and daunting, but without the following a CEO will be skating on even thinner ice than is really necessary:

- **The ability to think:** CEOs need seasoned judgment, visionary thinking, financial acumen and a global perspective in order to do their jobs.
- **Strategic management:** They need to be able to shape strategy, drive execution, and measure performance.
- **Leadership:** CEOs need to attract and develop talent, empower others, influence and negotiate, and be versatile in their leadership styles.
- **Interpersonal:** They need to build relationships within the organisation and to inspire trust within their people.
- **Communication:** Their strengths should include fostering open dialogue, public presentation skills and articulation.

- **Motivation:** CEOs have to be able to foster drive within themselves, and engender a hunger for entrepreneurial risk-taking and business success.
- **Self-management:** CEOs need a mature confidence, discipline, adaptability, career direction and self-direction.
- **Breadth and depth:** They must have cross-functional capacity and an in-depth understanding of the dynamics of their industry.

These skills are what I like to refer to as the tick-box stuff. Every successful business leader has to have them, and to continuously work on them in order to smooth the way to business success.

In *Maslow on Management*, Abraham Maslow outlined the qualities of the Superior Manager:

> *Sees most human beings as having real*
> *capacity for growth and development, for*
> *the acceptance of responsibility, for creative*
> *accomplishments.*

Maslow goes on to claim that it is a matter of *evolution*: less evolved beings are the ones who display the aggression, antagonism, disrespect and contempt for their colleagues, and that this will put them at a disadvantage in the marketplace as it too becomes more evolved.

> *The more evolved people get, the more*
> *psychologically healthy they get, the more*

will enlightened management policy be necessary.

As the war for talent wages, and as businesses increasingly recognise that the key to success is their ability to attract and retain good people, they are going to have to figure out that a large salary is only one part of an attractive job offer. The ability to realise dreams, to achieve the ideal of a balanced life, and to feel as if they are contributing to the greater good will be much more important components of the employment contract into the future. To truly understand this, CEOs have no choice but to start with themselves.

YOUR PERSONAL STATE

The last of the three factors that combine to enable a person to achieve sustainable success is his or her personal state. Much of my work has been involved in developing this, the most nebulous of factors – working with CEOs to prevent them sacrificing the balance and joy that is available to them outside the workplace that can reflect so beneficially on their performance within it.

For many business leaders, focusing on the personal can be an intensely uncomfortable experience. To succeed in the modern world of business, many people make real sacrifices, often without even realising it, and it is only when they begin to ask themselves serious questions about the nature of their success that they realise what they have done.

An individual's personal state is dependent on many factors, many of them hidden within their own psyche. Successful business executives are by their very nature driven and ambitious. Research shows that often male CEOs are first-born children, and surprisingly frequently they have had a father figure who was absent or distant, but a warm and supportive mother. A former CEO of GE, Jack Welch, for instance, writes in his autobiography about his powerhouse of a mother and depicts his father, a train conductor, as pleasant enough but not very present. Richard Branson was the same, and Bill Clinton's father died before he was born. Sigmund Freud even said that there is nothing as conducive to success as being your mother's favourite.

To achieve a state of sustainable success, it is crucial that an individual understands the underlying drives that motivate them, and comes to terms with any past issues that may be influencing their behaviours, attitudes or values. Psychotherapy or analysis may be useful, but it might simply be that space for self-reflection and growth is needed.

As well as understanding and coming to terms with your own drives and motivations, it is also important to develop a healthy and balanced life outside the workplace. Personal relationships need to be strong and supportive to carry you through the stresses of life, with your partner, your children, your friends and relatives. I also think it is crucial to have interests outside of the workplace such as hobbies, an area of study or a means of expression that is not work- or family-related but that brings you a sense of peace and perspective. In addition, involvement in community life – a local charity perhaps, your children's school or the neighbourhood council – has a remarkable ability to generate feelings of involvement, and the knowledge that you are giving back in return for your own success and good fortune.

ERIKSON'S COMFORT WITH LIFE

According to psychologist Erik Erikson, people develop through eight stages in life. Each stage consists of a crisis that must be faced – not a catastrophe but a turning point of increased vulnerability and enhanced potential. The more an individual resolves these crises successfully, the healthier development will be.

Most leaders hit their stride during what Erikson terms 'Middle Age'. Having developed intimate relationships during young adulthood and determined what our lives are about, during Middle Age we need to go beyond ourselves and our families an become involved in helping the next generation. Middle Age for many is a time of adjusting to the discrepancy between one's dreams and one's actual accomplishments; and developing real balance between work, family and community activities is one way of avoiding psychological stagnation and bitterness.

A healthy individual who manages to achieve balance can look forward to the next developmental stage: Later Life. According to Erikson, the core crisis of the elderly is integrity versus despair. Ego integrity is achieved by those who have few regrets, who have lived a productive and worthwhile life and have coped with failures as well as successes. They are not obsessed with what might have been, and can derive satisfaction from what they have done. Those who can't do this tend to have feelings of despair, hopelessness, guilt, resentment and self-disgust.

Ego integrity, for my money, is as good a definition of success as any I have come across.

AVOIDING SPILLOVER

Fernando Bartolome and Paul Lee Evans, two professors at European business school INSEAD, studied the professional and private lives of some 2000 managers for nearly five years. The study's goal was to determine what differentiated those executives who successfully managed to balance their professional lives from those who paid a personal price for their professional success. The findings appeared later in the *Harvard Business Review*:

> *The executives whose private lives deteriorate are subject to the negative effects of what we call emotional spillover; work consistently produces negative feelings that overflow into private life.*

Fundamentally, the executive who is unhappy in their work 'has a limited chance of being happy at home'. When work is going well, when people are challenged by what they do in the right measure, it can have the same effect as healthy physical exercise: instead of leading to fatigue, it is invigorating, and there is plenty of positive spillover energy left for the family. When things are going badly, the opposite is true. People in the wrong jobs have real trouble managing their home lives, because they are obsessed with what has been going on in the workplace even when they do come home.

Bartolome and Lee Evans claimed their research showed that people need to understand the importance of managing their careers in a way that will allow them to bring energy and life back home with them, but importantly, it is also up to companies to provide them with an environment in which this is possible.

This fits neatly with the issues I outlined in the 'Corporate culture' chapter. Companies that manage their people badly, who do not provide them with empowered roles or challenge them to a sufficient extent, and workplaces that are dominated by power politics and the language of abuse are the most likely to result in poor home lives for their people. Bartolome and Lee Evans suggest that organisations can actively prevent burdening their people with negative spillover through several initiatives:

- **Broaden organisational values:** Encourage people not to be solely devoted to career success. This is something I have promoted throughout my career, from my earliest days at Microsoft. Sure, I felt, doing a good job in the workplace is crucial, but realistically, whatever you do in the workplace is just *work*. The important stuff goes on in the rest our lives. Being committed to your company doesn't mean that you need to sacrifice everything for it, and demanding commitment from your people doesn't mean you can demand their presence in the office at midnight every night.

- **Create multiple reward and career ladders:** Offering simple, hierarchical reward structures encourages people into the wrong jobs. People need to be rewarded appropriately for their contribution to the organisation.

- **Give realistic performance appraisals:** Managers need to be realistic with their people to avoid pushing them into roles that don't fit, or promoting them to their 'Peter principle' level of incompetence. They need to encourage self-assessment that focuses on the extent to which people enjoy their jobs. Be realistic about a person's chances of promotion or their fitness for particular jobs.

- **Reduce organisational uncertainty:** Of course, uncertainty is part of life. The business environment, as we are so used to hearing, is becoming even more uncertain. Terrorism, recession, technological developments – these things and many more make the business environment complex. But Bartolome and Lee Evans say that it is up to managers to protect their subordinates from uncertainty and trust them to do their jobs. By absorbing pressures about which your people can do nothing, you make it more possible for people to do their jobs in a satisfying way, and to balance their own lives, which in turn will bring energy back into the workplace. To that I would add communication. We all know that knowledge is a panacea for uncertainty, and even if you are unable to tell your people everything that is going on, you owe it to them to tell them as much as you can so that they are able to manage their lives as effectively as possible.

THE SUSTAINABLE LEADER

So with all of this, what would a sustainable leader actually look like? For me there are several characteristics that executives need to work towards in order to achieve the idea of sustainable leadership.

Firstly, and crucially, they must understand themselves. They must know their personality and how it behaves in different situations, they must know their own attitudes, understand their values – what is important in life and in business, and what is not – and their beliefs. Importantly, too, they must have consistent and dependable integrity. When they say they are going to do something, they should do it. When they make a promise, they should keep it. And when faced with an ethical choice, they should recognise it.

Sustainable leaders need to develop and reward competence, rather than considering talented people rivals or threats, and actively search out people with greater skills and bring them into the fold. They should cherish diversity and recognise that people with different backgrounds bring different and valuable perspectives to the situation. When presented with contrary opinions they should be open to them, rather than shutting them out.

Sustainable leaders are able to communicate easily at all levels, they can engage in complex and detailed discussions if necessary or make difficult subjects simple when explaining them to people who have a simpler level of understanding. They advocate equity within the organisation, similar treatment for similar performance, rather than playing favourites. They have a deep understanding of the organisation, how it works, how it creates value, its relationships with customers and suppliers, and between its departments. They have a vision for the organisation, and an implementable strategy to achieve it. And they are deeply committed to the company's employees and to its shareholders for the long term.

As well as all of this, sustainable leaders understand that life has many aspects to it, and work is just one of these, for themselves and for their employees. While passionate about what they do and the work of their organisation, these leaders see work in perspective and they do not lose sight of what really matters to themselves and to their staff.

Success is measured by more than one yardstick, and it is defined by the inner state of the individual and his or her level of satisfaction in life as a *human being* rather than simply as a businessperson. How can a CEO whose personal life is a train wreck, who has no friends, who has forgotten who they are, and who cannot function outside the artificial structures of the workplace call themselves successful?

THE SECRET STUFF

All of this brings us to an uncomfortable place. What is it that we really want? At the risk of being completely unfashionable, and being ostracised even further from the macho Australian business culture, I am going to lay it on the line: **We all want to feel a sense of belonging. We all want to be loved. We all want to be cared for and to care for others. More than this, people obsessed with work end up lonely, sad, bitter souls.**

In *Well & Good*, Eckersley provides an entree to the work of Canadian psychologist Bruce Alexander, who argued that psychological integration – the individual's experience of belonging, and being accepted and understood – is what makes life bearable, even joyful. Modern, free-market societies systematically promote its opposite, and 'dislocate' individuals from traditional sources of psychological, social and spiritual support. Dislocated people struggle to find or restore pyschological integration (to somehow 'get a life') and eventually construct lifestyles that substitute for it – lifestyles that are based on addiction to a few pursuits, to the detriment of a broader, more balanced life.

I don't think that the people who lead our great public corporations are bad people. I think they have been moulded by their environments, caught up in circumstances, and very often lose sight of themselves.

They have the same need for belonging, but unfortunately they end up belonging to a group of similarly dysfunctional people, where the sense of belonging requires living a life that does not bring happiness or fulfilment but rather demands excessive focus on work and its rewards. If this set of people were to take these issues in hand and consciously work towards developing a more sustainable brand of leadership, it would be a great boon for their own lives and, through the cultures of their organisations, for a great portion of society as well.

It is a big secret, nobody seems to be talking about it, but you *can* have it all. But only if you are prepared to work towards balance and let go of those things that do not matter. Once that is achieved, manage your people as you would want to be managed.

A life of sustained success means more than simply filling up the cupboard with money. It means good health; long-term financial rewards; national, industry and peer recognition of your achievement; opportunities to develop and grow, and to help others develop and grow; healthy friendships and family relationships; well-developed personal interests; and a strong and enduring social legacy. It is possible, and it is up to you.

PART III

BUILDING A PLATFORM FOR YOUR LIFE

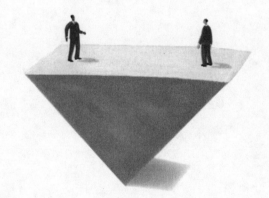

07

YOUR CAREER

In my first job in the computer industry, working for Burroughs, the company encouraged a number of its people to specialise in a particular technical area. In most cases this meant becoming a specialist in a programming language or systems design approach that only applied to specific Burroughs computers. It is important to remember that at this time, the late 1970s and early 1980s, PCs had not yet appeared in any volume and the computer industry was dominated by mainframe and minicomputer vendors who each marketed a completely proprietary hardware and software solution. IBM, DEC, Honeywell, Burroughs, Sperry Univac and Wang made up the big end of town in the 1980 computer industry. I was never particularly enthusiastic about becoming involved in such a highly technical area, and preferred to focus on the market-facing side of the business, talking to clients and marketing products. I felt that, although I was involved in the marketing of proprietary products, the actual skills involved were universally applicable to any technology product or vendor.

My colleague John, however, was enthusiastic about the technical side, and eventually became the country's leading specialist in the programming of a particular minicomputer range called the B90. He became an extremely valuable resource. He knew everything there was to know about the system, his position was well respected, he was paid a lot of money and attracted a lot of praise and encouragement from management. At the time, John enjoyed it all. His job was challenging and he was receiving all sorts of positive reinforcement. Within several years, though, he had found himself in something of a career cul-de-sac. His problem was that he was too specialised, and his skills were only appropriate for that particular position in that particular company. There was no way he could move to another job in another company and get paid a similar amount. The risk John was running, while he raked in his specialist fees, was that as the industry changed, his skills would become increasingly niche, and increasingly redundant. And that, of course, is what happened.

Even at the time I would say to him, 'Don't you think you ought to broaden your skills base a little more?' But he always replied that this is what the company wanted of him, that he was earning very good money being a global specialist and that the company would look after him. He never gave any thought to his marketability outside of

Burroughs in the broader IT industry or whether his skills were applicable to other industries. Unfortunately, he allowed recognition from his employer to cloud his ability to think about employment as purely a transaction, one that was currently stacked in the favour of his employer.

The same was true of Marcus, another friend of mine, who was in a senior sales role at a multinational company, selling a particular kind of financial services software to large national financial institutions. Whenever I would ask him about his life, he would always talk about his dedication to the firm, and the faith he had that the company would look after him. For many years it did look after him. He was paid very well, transferred all over the world, and he achieved great things in his line of business. The problem was that when his line of business ran out, he looked up from his career cocoon to find that he didn't know where he was going next. For Marcus, the tragedy of overspecialisation was compounded by the fact that he did it all at the expense of his home life. His wife and children barely knew him, and he barely knew them.

I have written about my last work interaction with Marcus a number of times, and the event is something I will never forget. We were sitting on the third floor of the company's Sydney headquarters at around 5.30 pm. I was 23 at the time and he would have been in his late forties. Minutes earlier he had been called into the national sales manager's office and told he was being made redundant. It seemed the Australian market (and the rest of the financial industry globally) was no longer interested in the specific solution that Marcus was expert in.

Marcus was one of those type of sales people whose schmooze factor is low but whose product knowledge impresses clients. As we sat and chatted, he talked about how much he had given the company, moving countries every three or four years over a twenty-year period of employment. How the constant uplifting and horrendous work schedules had created a void between himself and his family, and how all he needed was another few good years to be able to retire. Yet now it was all gone. He believed that his skills were not easily transportable and that as a result there was no way he could get another role on a similar salary package. At that time in my life I had never seen a grown man cry and when he started quietly sobbing as he cleaned out his desk, I felt so desperately sorry for him. I resolved that I would never let myself get into the position that Marcus had.

In the short term, John and Marcus's companies did do the right thing by them, yet with a clear main focus on what was right for the organisation. They paid them well and gave them interesting work. It would be easy to paint these companies as bad guys but it would be inappropriate. Both John and Marcus were paid very well and they were never forced to continue on the career trajectories that they chose.

Perhaps one could argue that the organisations could have thought more about their long-term employment prospects and kept their skill sets broadly applicable in the IT industry. But do we really believe that it is an organisation's responsibility to ensure its employees have skill sets that make them marketable outside of the organisation? Companies are focused on producing performance, particularly in the short term. In these cases the companies' interests in the short term came to dominate John and Marcus's lives, and when the short term ended they hadn't planned anything. It was not the company's fault but their own.

Notwithstanding one of the messages in the previous chapter – how leaders can best produce results in the long term by worrying about the real needs of employees – the reality remains that most companies operate on very short planning cycles. Companies pay little regard to the issue of the long-term life needs of an employee (I am talking here about lifelong learning, constant marketability, etc, and not just generous superannuation).

These men had lost perspective on their relationship with their companies. They had allowed the *value equation* between them and their companies to become reversed.

YOUR VALUE EQUATION

Do you need your company more than your company needs you? If so, you are on the wrong side of the value equation. In money terms, could you get a job for the same money somewhere else? If the answer is no, they've got you.

Employment is a transaction. The company pays you a certain emolument in exchange for your labour, as defined in your contract of employment. At any point in time, that emolument will be above or below how much you are really worth to the company. The exact monetary figure might be difficult to determine, but intuitively we all know if we are being paid too much or too little. A simple test is to imagine what other jobs you might get that would pay a similar amount. If there aren't any, then you are being overpaid – at least as far as your employment equation is concerned.

If you are being paid too much, it becomes very difficult for you to consider alternative employment arrangements. On the other hand, if you are being paid too little (as far as your employment value is concerned), the company needs you more than you need it, and it becomes more difficult for the company to override your personal priorities.

I am not suggesting that you storm in to your boss or the board and demand a salary cut. In terms of your personal value to the company, the actual level of your salary is neither here nor there. What is important is that you think of yourself as a saleable asset whose value can be increased or decreased by your own actions. I *am* suggesting that you actively work on your personal value to your employer and to the market generally. How relevant and valuable are your skills to the company and the broader employment market, now and in the future? How can you make your skills more relevant in order to actively increase your value to employers now and in the future? What career building skills are you developing at the moment?

Equally important is a cold analysis of your industry and your company's place in it. What will the industry look like in five years time, and what will your company's role in it be? Will the industry have grown or shrunk? Will it have consolidated or fragmented? What will be the position of your product or service, and how will your company position its offerings to take advantage of the new landscape.

Some of my better career decisions have been taken after cool consideration of the nature of the changes within my industry and how best to take advantage of those changes. I went from computer hardware to computer software as it became evident that hardware was fast becoming a commodity. I went into the internet industry as it became clear that, although high risk, internet ventures could be viable, sustainable businesses. Each decision was a risky one, but I took them having at least looked at the factors that might influence their success or not.

Too many people simply make decisions – even risky ones – without recognising that they have made any decision at all. Others make, effectively, huge decisions by not doing any analysis of their current industry and employer. By *not* doing any analysis, they are intuitively saying that they are in the best possible career position in the industry with the most (or at least, more than some) opportunities.

Career risk exists whether you understand the nature of that risk or not. If you do not take the time to think about your career and its progression, your industry and your company's place within it, then you run the risk of waking up one day to find everything shifted from under you. If, on the other hand, you do take the time to consider these things you run the risk of discovering that you are completely out of your comfort zone and have to objectively question and quantify how marketable you are as a person. It's a scary choice.

But, just as we cannot rely on our partners to manage our own relationships with our children, we cannot rely on anyone to manage our work relationships. The modern career *is* frightening and challenging precisely because we have to do it ourselves . . . Being a grown-up is scary.

In Chapter 3 I wrote about the Petre principle: 'In a haphazardly structured career we take on roles that pay a lot more than we can earn elsewhere, and rather than put this away we increase our lifestyle to map our income level.' There is no law that says that we must be trapped by the Petre principle. We are self-determining individuals, with greater freedom in our lives than we admit to ourselves. Taking control of your own life and career is frightening and 'out there', but it might be the single most important factor between those who lead truly successful lives and those who find themselves in unexpected and unpleasant life situations.

DECIDING WHAT REALLY MATTERS TO YOU

What do you care about? What do you dream about? What do you really want? If you find it difficult to come up with answers to these questions off the top of your head, you're not the only one.

When I ask people these questions in seminars, (mostly career seminars where people have been sent by their employer), they also have a hard time answering. The first thing out of their mouths is usually something like: 'I want to double the number of active client relationships we have within ten months, triple our sales volume by the end of the financial year, and double profits in eighteen months.'

'No,' I respond, 'what I'm after is what you *really* want. What it is that you work for, what real satisfaction at work means for you. Where does your sense of purpose come from? Are you doing something fulfilling?'

Richard Eckersley, discussing the meaning of life in *Well & Good*, reported on Australian researchers Bruce Headey and Alex Wearing's findings that 'sense of meaning and purpose is the single attitude most strongly associated with life satisfaction'. Eckersley took meaning to include 'self-transcendent values, strong religious beliefs, membership of groups, dedication to a cause and clear life goals'.

However much you try to spin this concept of the meaning of life, it is difficult for the majority to use it to define the meaning in our life purely by our work. Our work may provide self-esteem, financial reward and sense of purpose but on its own it fails to provide true meaning to our lives.

After unpeeling layer after layer – onion-like – of other people's expectations, things they think you want to hear, and other diversionary tactics, occasionally you might find that people still harbour hopes, dreams and aspirations. It is difficult enough for people to admit this to themselves, let alone speak it out loud in a work-based seminar. Too often these hopes, dreams and aspirations are buried under layers: I hope my family doesn't implode, I hope we can make the mortgage payments, and other stuff from our complex daily lives.

The question is why this need be so. Kids have hopes and dreams and imaginations, but adulthood squeezes them all out. Something goes wrong somewhere along the way. The same is true of balance in our lives. When we are kids, balance in our lives is forced on us. Good parents will make sure that we don't spend too much of the day doing any one thing, whether that be studying or playing or watching television, or whatever. Children are usually encouraged to seek out joy in simple things like the smell of flowers or the cool splash of water or the whoosh of a kite. This emphasis on balance continues throughout our early adulthood. When we go to university, we might study hard, but it is a sad student who doesn't spend plenty of time in the student union, playing sport or having some sort of fun.

Then we start work and it all begins to go pear-shaped. Suddenly we are dedicating the bulk of our waking hours and all of our energy to one activity only, and nothing else in our lives is supposed to matter. We are told that if we want a career, this is the way it is. Even though it is so counterintuitive to everything we have done in our lives up until now, social pressures are such that we just seem to accept it. We get sucked in and over time forget about the other stuff we used to have in our lives: joy, balance, and many different interests and relationships outside of the workplace.

Suddenly the group we belong to (our work colleagues) seem to also accept the way it is, and to remain a group member (and get paid!), we continue to behave like the rest even though deep down we know that such an existence is not a life and not what we want out of life. To rebel, however, is to put yourself outside your group, and this is a lonely and uncomfortable place to be. To risk your job is

unthinkable – especially if you have significant commitments – and so you cope, and over time coping becomes the
accepted lifestyle.

In *The Reflecting Glass*, leadership coaches Lucy
West and Mike Milan ask their readers to take time to
think deeply about what really matters to them. They
provide a useful pie chart that breaks down the thinking
process to ensure we focus on all aspects of 'what really
matters to us'.

When I first came across this tool I found some of
the areas quite disconcerting. In particular the concept of
articulating hopes, dreams and aspirations, and to express
these without constantly referring to my career. This process
brought into sharp focus the fact that I actually rarely spent
time thinking about aspirations outside of work and that I

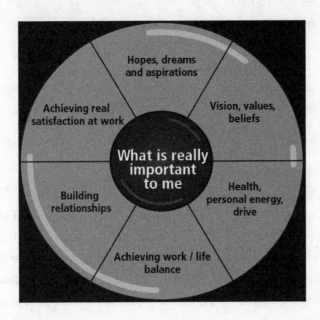

did not have dreams in the way a small child might. They will dream of an idea that is completely removed from pragmatic analysis and yet it is this ability to be inspired outside of what is pragmatic that allows us to truly grow.

Really focusing on what matters is difficult because it goes to the core of who we are, how we live our lives, and what our lives are really about. To ask 'What am I all about?' is one of the most powerful and important steps you can take as an adult. It is about being *self-aware*.

Self-awareness means that you:

- have a clear understanding of reality
- have the ability to handle uncertainty
- have the ability to respond spontaneously
- are comfortable with your surroundings
- are creative
- accept yourself
- are independent
- understand how your behaviour impacts on others
- are able to give love
- can deal with the problems of others – you are not self-centred
- have a zest for living
- enjoy others but can also enjoy serenity
- have a purpose in life.

Theories about enlightened management all stem from this point: people are more than entities that consume food and drink and create energy. We all have a life force, a reason for being, an actual self which we strive to achieve. The more we work towards this goal, the happier and more productive we become. But it stands to reason that the only way we can do this is to ask the questions of ourselves in the first place: What really matters to me? What do I really want?

ORGANISATIONS, YOUR CAREER AND YOURSELF

Our careers, and our ability to realise ourselves through them, are heavily influenced by the organisations that employ us. To plan a career we need to take a close look at the nature of those organisations and be realistic about the environment in which that career will develop. As we saw in the 'Corporate culture' chapter, many of the organisations we work for are severely dysfunctional. It starts at the top, with the CEOs the role models for the rest of the organisation, lest we forget.

The fundamental problem is that the CEOs and top management in dysfunctional organisations are from a different time and place. Often they simply have fundamentally different conditioning, values and ideals from their people. At the tail ends of their careers, they have often lived their life, they have made their work/life choices and are not in the same place as those of us who are still working these things out. By their stage in life, most CEOs have forgotten what it is like to struggle with small kids in the morning who do not want to go to school, how maintaining a relationship takes time and energy, and how financial pressure can distort decisions. In short, they are in a different place from most of their people, and their behaviour and understanding is appropriate to their own time of life. Many gave up having a normal life decades ago, and their frame of reference simply does not take into account a broader life and set of interests.

Having spent twenty or thirty years inside the corporation, many business leaders have become the company. How many times have you seen a CEO on television lying through their teeth, justifying some deplorable act on behalf of their company? Either they believe their own lies or they are dealing with horrendous internal conflicts.

Many people make the mistake of thinking that their leaders or the organisations they work for are going to change, that they will be able to get on with their own lives once things around here are sorted. But CEOs are just people – and changing people is as hard as changing an organisation. There are few motivations for dysfunctional CEOs to change: the only reason they might is if they were to remember the pain of losing their children through neglect, or if they were to remember the passion they had for life when they were younger. Fat chance, to be honest.

The message is that you shouldn't wait around for your CEO or the organisation to change. Fundamentally, the environment in many organisations is simply not encouraging of balance. But it is your life, your journey and your career. You have to own it for yourself and you may be disappointed if you expect your organisation to understand – because we know that so many of them do not. At the same time, as we saw in Chapter 5, people are more productive in companies that do provide a supportive and open environment. There is good data showing that people who believe in what they are doing work hard and are happy to do so. We know for a fact that people who are given autonomy and responsibility are more likely to be productive and stay with the organisation. It is a serious injustice that more organisations don't take this approach to managing their people.

CHOOSING AN EMPLOYER

You've done the hard work and thought about what matters to you. You've done the organisational diagnostic and determined the kind of organisation that you want to work for. The question then becomes, how do you chose an employer? The answer depends on what stage in your career you are at.

Early career choice

Early in your career it is important to look for a company that will allow you to develop a wide range of skills and involve you in a wide range of experiences – perhaps an organisation that rotates its people between local and overseas assignments or between different departments. This helps you to develop your marketability, but at this stage it also provides you with a broad range of experiences and gives you more ideas about your future.

It is also important that you carefully choose the kind of leader that you want to work with. Finding a great leader early in your career – as I was lucky enough to do with Bill Gates – is probably the best thing you can do.

Once you have chosen your company, try to find a mentor – someone who can help you learn about life in the corporate world, steer you through complex situations, and help you through the crises that will arise.

Equally important is to look for a company that you can believe in. Do you think the industry is adding value to society, or does it destroy it? Would you be happy to tell your kids that you work in that industry?

Try to pick a company that is, or is likely to become, the best in the industry. Why? Because that is where, more often than not, the best people will be. Be careful here to choose best and not necessarily biggest. Take telecommunications in Australia as an example. Telstra is far and away the biggest corporation in this space but a long way from being regarded as the best performer.

I was lucky enough to be able to work for the company that was far and away the best in its industry at a time when that industry was growing and changing enormously. Some of the world's best and smartest IT people were working at Microsoft in the '80s and '90s, and just by working there along side some seriously talented people I was enhancing my skill set and adding to my side of the employment equation.

Mid-career choice

The middle of your career is when you are developing into your own leadership role. It is a crucial time for laying the foundations for achieving your goals. It is at this time that you ought to be thinking about the legacy you would like to leave, about what really matters to you, about how you would like to change the world. In fifteen to twenty years, you will be leaving your main career. What would you like to think about it when it is over, and how can you make that happen?

This is a crucial stage for choosing your employer. Can you afford to choose a dying industry or a systematically flawed employer? As you head further into your career, mistakes like this become more expensive and wasteful.

This is not to say that you shouldn't take some risks with your middle career, but your career decisions should be taken carefully, with a view to minimising that risk. Going into the internet in the late 1990s was a risky proposition, but analysing how the internet industry was going to develop, understanding the ramifications of the sea-change that was going on in business, and choosing the right company helped me to minimise the risk I was taking.

As at any time in your working life, you need to look for an organisation that has values, a corporate culture and a leadership model that are aligned with your own – unless you realistically think that by joining the place you can change it. You want to be able to tell your children what you've been doing all day, and tell it proudly. You don't want to wake up one day and wonder why you've been working as a tobacco lawyer all your life.

Mentors are important throughout your career, and the availability of mentors should influence your choice of employer. Also, look for a place that will provide you with a reasonably rapid ability to broaden your skill base and increase the scope of your role. After all, you will need increased responsibilities to test and develop your management and leadership skills. Beware of the middle management trap – the last thing you want is to find that a peer manager is ten years younger than you and just as capable. You need to be thinking about how you are going to make your mark, and work towards that, rather than finding yourself on the middle management treadmill.

It is just as important to continually enhance your skill base. Having done an analysis of your career, you may find that you are somewhere you completely do not want to be, in a dying industry or doing something you hate. You may find that you will need to re-tool your entire skill set in order to be where you want to be in five years time. What is important is that you realise this and take control of things before they slip even further.

At this time it is crucial to actively develop your external network. One aspect of leadership is getting things done, and *people* are the only way to get things done. Making and maintaining connections now will be a big help as you work towards making your mark.

This may be the time to begin laying the foundations for a portfolio career, where you are not dependent on one employer but on a network of clients who employ you for freelance projects that take advantage of your skill set. By developing other sources of employment and income outside of your main employment, you weaken your employer's power over you and multiply your degrees of freedom.

The portfolio career will become more and more common, especially as people move into 'semi-retirement' or retire from their full-time employment at an age that will mean they still have twenty or thirty healthy and virile working years. As we live longer and longer lives, retiring at 65 will simply mean that the still-virile executive will leave permanent employment and embark on a consulting career for twenty years or so. The middle of your career is when you need to begin developing your ideas about what your late career will be about.

It is also crucial at this time that you lay the financial future for yourself and your family. As we will see in the next chapter, that involves realistic financial planning.

Late career choice

As your career progresses, you ought to have a clearer view of what your legacy should be. You need to look for organisations to which you feel you will be able to add value until very late in your career. Having done that, your job is to focus on what you will need to do to leave the organisation, and the people who are in it, better off for your having been there.

Having said that, it is just as easy to sell your soul – to trade away your own goals for those of the organisation, to work towards the wrong goals – late in your career as it is in the beginning. You need to ensure that there will be opportunities for you to develop your external network; you need to be thinking about what you are going to be doing after you have left this company and are moving into your 'portfolio phase'. Lifelong learning means you will still need to be developing your marketable skills that will offer you the opportunity to diversify and take advantage of a broader range of options as your career changes.

This is the period in your career where you ought to have the chance to give back to others, to become a mentor to the younger generation. Many leaders report to me that this is one of the most satisfying aspects of being in the later stage of their career, living their people's victories and defeats with them and lending them vital experience.

A REALITY CHECK

All this talk of hopes, dreams, aspirations, values, corporate culture and balance is well and good, but we already know that most organisations don't live by this creed. Companies exist to make money for their shareholders, and that is what most managers focus on.

In an ideal world, companies would care for their employees, have a high level of social responsibility, and develop reasonable business plans that have sustainability. If you find a company that does all these things, that is fantastic. But most do not – many *say* they do, but actually don't. Early twenty-first century capitalism is structured against these ideas: markets are focused on quarterly earnings results and do not reward companies for their long-term people and sustainability values, especially if they are seen to lower short-term profits.

How many value statements have you seen that don't in any way relate to the actual values that are displayed by the leaders of the organisation and the way the company does business? Companies are awash with meaningless values statements that do not in any way influence the way that behaviours are rewarded.

What we can hope for, and work towards, is some sort of corporate realisation. If we say it enough and behave as if that is what we really believe, companies might accept that the health of the individual and the health of the organisation they work for is linked.

We can hope that companies will develop an enlightened management model that does align the interests of the company with the interests and wellbeing of the people who work there. We can hope that over time more and more companies might adopt a sustainable management culture. And we can hope that the ideas of command and control, the culture of burn-out and the values vacuum that dominates many organisations now might slowly fade away.

TAKE CONTROL OF YOUR CAREER

As outlined earlier, when *Father Time* was published and I began talking about the idea of work–life balance, I was often shocked at the ferocity of anger that I would encounter from men who had taken exception to my message. Six years down the line, it seems to me that in each of these cases I had struck at a really tender spot for these men – many of whom had traded away their lives for money, power or other career ideals that were simply not as satisfying as living a full and varied life.

I would be angry if somebody were to point out to me that I had made consistently wrong choices in my life. It would hurt. But I hope that I would listen to what was being said and perhaps try to change things for the future.

This is your personal journey – it is your life. Every day you are making choices, even if you don't make any choices.

- Remember, by staying where you are, you are making the choice that this is where you want to be.
- By not enhancing your skills, you are making a choice that you do not need to enhance your skills, that your side of the employment equation is valuable enough.

- By not taking an objective view of your industry and your company's relative performance in it, you are making the choice to be uninformed, or to be taken by surprise.
- By not developing other strings to your bow – other streams of income, or other parts of your portfolio – you are choosing to depend on your main employer to fund your lifestyle.
- By ramping up your expenses to match your income, you are saying that you have multiple career choices providing the same income and that job security is no risk to your family's lifestyle.

The most important thing is to take control of your career because, in the end, the only person that will truly care about how your career progresses is you. This may be harsh and cynical but it is also painfully true.

Take control and *own* your career.

08

MONEY AND LIFE

'It's alright for you.' I cannot tell you how many times I've heard that refrain from people when I begin to discuss the subject of work–life balance. It is alright for me, these people are saying, because from their perspective I have been financially successful and can therefore afford to kick back, to work 'part time' and to seek balance. Others, less financially well off, are doomed to a life of slavery, apparently, spending long hours in the office just to bring home enough bacon to support their modest needs.

This is partly true: there is no point talking about balance in your life and ensuring you live a complete and fulfilled existence unless you have a roof over your head, clothes on your back, and food in your stomach. Even Abraham Maslow, the guru of enlightened management, recognised that until our baser needs are met, we are not free to pursue the higher purposes of our existence. However, I think it's fair to say that many of the highly paid executives who come out with this response have a very stable financial platform for their life, by any reasonable measure.

I do admit that it is not fair to expect someone who is really struggling to be able to engage in a conversation about balance. The irony is that it is often the work practices of the wealthy, financially stable senior executives that create the debilitating working conditions for those employees that have little financial stability and are struggling to exist.

The difficulty is how to retain perspective on what is a required financial platform to fund a life you really want to lead, as opposed to a life built on acquiring things that make you look good in the eyes of others. This is easy to say and yet hard to do. It is hard because at every turn someone or some business is suggesting that you will be that little bit happier/sexier/more successful/more accepted if you just purchased this or that item. It is easy to get caught up in the race for more, and yet, deep down, we all know that above a certain level of comfort (which is different for all people) we do not actually get more happiness from the next thing.

In some parts of society we will be more accepted because of where we live, what car we drive or where we work. On reflection, do we really want to be included in a group that has as its primary membership criteria some material asset? It is this unfortunate focus on getting more that leads us to work during every waking hour.

At the same time, there is a fundamental difference between working hard and working smart, and this can be the deciding factor between attaining sustainable success and looking back and wondering where your life has gone. People who understand their needs, have concrete and realistic financial goals, and understand how they will attain them, have a greater chance of liberating themselves from the tyranny of the dollar and being able to devote themselves to more worthwhile and varied pursuits.

THE QUESTION OF FINANCIAL SECURITY

In the 'Work and life' chapter I wrote about the firm that pays its people 30 to 70 per cent above its competitors in exchange for its pound of flesh. It amazes me how many of those fortunate enough to land such a lucrative job don't use it as a ticket to early financial freedom, but as an extra yoke to tie themselves into the company and the long-hours lifestyle. Instead of paying off a nice house, boat and car while they're raking in the extra cash, these employees use every opportunity to upgrade their commitments and leverage themselves to the hilt. Even though they are extremely financially well off, they are not free, simply because they haven't taken the time to think about what their real needs are, and how they can be met through a sound and well-planned financial life strategy.

Financial insecurity is a fundamental fear that drives us through our working lives, but there is a serious question as to whether this fear is real or whether we imagine it. The truth is that at the beginning of the twenty-first century, Australia is one of the world's best economies, and we live one of the world's best lifestyles.

Less than 1 per cent of houses in Australia do not have a fridge; less then 2 per cent don't have a landline telephone. A house without a television is rarer than hen's teeth. In 1997, 56 per cent had more than one TV and 82 per cent had a VCR. Just under 90 per cent of households had a car, and almost half have more than one. By 2000, more than half of all homes had a personal computer, a third of which were connected to the internet. We have purchased over 14 million mobile phones, and DVD players are now outstripping VCRs and being sold in their hundreds of thousands. Compare this existence to the rest of the world and we see that the significant majority of Australians live better than 95 per cent of the people inhabiting this planet.

Against this background, it is difficult to understand how financial insecurity comes to dominate so much of our public and private debate. The reason is because we have become fixated on relative wealth, rather than absolute wealth. All too often, the reason people enter into financial commitments that keep them locked into an unbalanced lifestyle is because, consciously or not, they want to show their relative success to others: 'Look at how successful I am – my house is bigger than yours.' Relative wealth is measured in toys and money, while absolute wealth is measured in all sorts of different ways: family, friends, relationships, health, lifestyle, and all the things that add up to a balanced life. It's all about perspective.

At a recent corporate function I met a new employee. After we'd exchanged names, the conversation became distinctly one-way, during which he seemed to list every asset he had. He talked about a holiday the family were planning in Queensland on their boat. But rather than just say this, he said 'We'll be taking our 30-metre cruiser, which I bought recently for $X, up to Queensland again this year.' The rest of the conversation continued along these lines and it became very obvious that the point was not that he really liked the large boat, large house and everything else he had, but that he wanted me to know he was a success because he had all this stuff.

This person then told me how many hours he was working and how difficult it was to get time to see his kids – surprise, surprise. It seemed pretty clear that his view of financial security was a little distorted. I see many people who, the moment they have any free cash flow, immediately upgrade their house or car with little regard to whether the increase in debt is actually worthwhile. Rarely, it seems, do these people consider saving some of the money or limiting their expenses, moves that would ultimately give them a higher level of financial security.

Most people lose perspective and chase the accumulation of more and higher-cost assets regardless of whether they actually want or need these assets. If you really love cars, boats, bikes, whatever, and in having this asset you truly feel better within yourself, fine. But if you're acquiring the asset as a signpost to others that you are doing well, this is not so fine. The key is keeping a sense on what you *really* need to live the life you *really* want to live. This is the basis for starting to create a plan for financial security.

CREATING FINANCIAL SECURITY

Financial security, the ability to provide a reasonable living and confidence in your ability to enjoy it into the future, is the basic platform we require. From there, we can start to think about leading a more complete life.

I asked one of Australia's leading financial experts, David Koch, for some ideas on how to develop a sustainable financial plan. David is executive director of Palamedia Limited and the resident business and finance expert for the Seven and Prime TV networks. He is co-host of Seven's *Sunrise* program and hosts *Sky Business Report* on Australia's Sky News channel. David is a man who is incredibly busy but also manages to spend considerable time with his wife and family.

As one would expect, David's knowledge of money and business is extensive, as is his history in this sector. In a survey conducted by *Money Management* newspaper, his peers recognised David as one of the most influential people in the financial services industry.

It makes sense then that if anyone is going to advise us on how to create personal financial security, it should be David Koch.

DEVELOPING FINANCIAL SECURITY: THE DAVID KOCH REGIMEN

Stop complaining about how hard it is to make ends meet and start doing something about it! It will need discipline and commitment. Here are some financial resolutions to get you off on the right track:

- **I *will* save all my loose change**

This is a painless way to maintain a modest savings plan. A couple of dollars a day will become $20 a week and $1000 a year.

I have a mate in Brisbane who at the end of the day puts any $1 coin in a jar after he clears out his pockets at the end of each day. He started when his daughter was born and now, eight years later, his savings program has grown to $13 000. (Make sure you hide the jar from the rest of the family, though, so they don't raid it).

- **I *will* set a savings goal**

Paying off the mortgage as soon as possible or making contributions to superannuation are two of the best savings goals you can set. Concentrate on the mortgage first, and when that has gone, make super the priority. Savings devoted to mortgage repayments is equivalent to investing an 8 per cent after-tax return.

- **I *will* plan ahead for this year's tax return**

Tax is a major cost for investors and employees. Don't let your tax bill come as a surprise. Planning can be more effective if it starts in January, not June.

- **I *will* plan my tax affairs to maximise my wealth**

Tax planning is not just for the rich, and it can be simple. Here are some basic guidelines:

> Split income by putting surplus money into an interest-bearing account in the name of a non-working spouse.

> When investing in term deposits, make sure they mature in July, not June. You will then have a year after earning interest before any tax is due.

> Purchase shares in the name of someone who can best make use of the imputation credits that come with franked dividends – not a child under eighteen or non-working spouse who don't pay any tax, in other words.

• I *will* not be tempted by tax shelters

In June every year, many tax payers rush around looking for investments that allow them to make tax losses and reduce their overall tax bill. They are not worth it. The result is that the taxman loses 48 per cent and you may lose the rest.

• I *will* make sure all my life insurance needs are covered

Make sure you have adequate term-life cover and income protection so that you and your dependants won't suffer if the unthinkable should happen. Ensure that the amount of coverage is realistic and get rid of any unnecessary policies. Old endowment policies or others with investment components aren't generally worthwhile as investors can get better returns elsewhere.

• I *will* keep my nerve on the sharemarket

The sharemarket took a beating in 2001–02 and investors' share portfolios or managed funds looked pretty shabby. But those who hung in there in quality stocks did pretty well.

If the companies are generally sound, don't sell out and crystallise your losses. The market will bounce back and the share prices of good companies will recover. Look to invest with a medium- to long-term view, and don't worry about short-term fluctuations.

- **I *will* consider security before return**
The prospect of higher returns always comes with higher risk. You can't afford to lose all your capital, so invest in proven performers. Consider risk first and return second: earn a little less, but with more certainty.

- **I *will* not base my investment decisions on last year's results**
Investment cycles fluctuate from year to year. Those who invested heavily in shares in 2001 on the strength of the great returns of the previous year lost out badly.

- **I *will* spread my risk**
By diversifying your investment across a range of assets (property, shares, fixed interest), you will cover yourself against any volatility associated with any one class of asset. For example, if you have just paid off the mortgage, don't go out and buy an investment property – spread the risk around.

GETTING YOUR FAMILY FINANCES UNDER CONTROL: THE KOCH FAMILY CRISIS

It's funny but no matter how much we earn, it never seems to be enough. As you get older you remember with amazement how you used to survive on such a meagre salary. Today, you are paid so much more and still have nothing left.

Sound familiar? It certainly was with the Koch family. Let me tell you from the start: finance journalists are the worst at handling their own money. It's a bit like the bootmaker always wearing the worst shoes. Married, four young children, mortgage, single income, the Koch family couldn't save a cracker. Libby cut the kids' pocket money in half during downturns and even the dog was put on half rations. Chaos ensued, the kids revolted: we had lost control of our finances . . .

We called the infamous Koch economic summit to work out the problem. We put the case about household expenses, the kids put forward a submission for a return to their old rates of pay, and we fell back on the old 'Money doesn't grow on trees' lecture.

It soon became clear that we had no idea where our money went. For years we'd talked about doing a family budget but had never actually sat down and done the sums. The result was an eight-point survival plan to take control of the finances:

1. Put the kids to bed
No distractions. This is serious stuff. Put aside a night, after the kids have gone to bed, to start your search for that elusive savings dollar. Clear the dining table and grab all the cheque books, credit card accounts, bank statements and pay slips.
2. List your income
This is the easy bit because it's generally the shortest

list. Get yourself a blank piece of paper and make a column for each month.

On the left side of the page list all the income you expect to receive: wages, maintenance, pensions, dividends, interest . . . everything. Then fill in the amount relevant for each month. Many banks have family budget papers in a number of their brochures which will save you drawing up your own schedule.

3. List your expenses

This is frightening and is the most common cause of budget-night friction as each spouse reels in horror at the expenses of the other. You'd better make a pact before proceedings start that there will be no recriminations for past spending patterns.

List your fixed expenses, the essential bills that are unavoidable. These would be the mortgage repayments, electricity, gas, phone, rates, car rego and insurance, rent or board, household insurances, and so on. Make sure you put them in the months when they need to be paid, to give an idea of which months will be leaner than others. You should plan to put some money aside from the 'good months' to cover the lean ones.

So far so good. Now comes the tricky bit because there is more to life than just electricity and phone bills. How much are you spending on food, fuel, bus fares, lunches, haircuts, cigarettes, alcohol, toiletries, CDs, doctors, dentists, newspapers and magazines? How much on birthday presents, clothes, school equipment, loan repayments, credit cards, household items, chemists, pocket money, and so on?

You have to be ruthless and honest with yourself. After all, the reason for doing a budget is to ensure that you have enough for the important things, and to isolate where you are wasting money. If you find it hard, discipline yourself for two weeks to write down every time you take money out of your wallet. You will be surprised at the number of times you open it for little things.

But be realistic. You shouldn't feel guilty about treating yourself to a cappuccino every now and then. At the end of listing our income and expenses we ended up with a deficit. It was a frightening reality but we pushed on regardless.

4. Cut down on luxuries

Another sensitive issue. One person's idea of a luxury is another's essential. But look at this area dispassionately because it is generally where the most savings can be made. Instead of regularly heading off to the movies or dinner, we entertain a lot more at home. The old-fashioned card nights, videos and board games have made a fun and cheap return to the Koch household.

Set yourself a monthly entertainment budget and make sure you stick with it.

5. Cut up the credit cards

Open your purse or wallet and marvel at the array of credit cards which seem to be on a mass-breeding program. Yes, they are convenient but they are also expensive. Do you know the interest rate on some of the store credit cards is as high as 24 per cent? Make enquiries, and for emergencies a keep one card which has an interest-free period. Cancel the rest of the cards and make sure you pay the balance of the remaining one on time.

6. Pay off any debts

You cannot save if you still owe money. So pay off that personal loan or overdraft. The interest rates are high and you can't afford it.

7. Review your insurance policies

We found that insurance premiums were a huge expense. But the biggest mistake you can make is to cut them out. Insurance is an essential safeguard against catastrophies and must be maintained even during tough times.

How many of us review our insurance policies to ensure we are getting value for money? Libby rang around the competitors of the insurers we had, and in many cases we could get the same cover and conditions at a cheaper premium.

8. Set a savings budget

If we saved what was left at the end of the month, we would have a tough battle. So what we did was set a savings budget where we take out a set amount at the start of the month when my wages are paid; our savings target is put away before we start spending.

One year later we'd ended up with some money in the bank. We'd paid off a bit extra from our mortgage, the kids were back on full allowance and the dog looked healthier. We reviewed our annual budget and even started a new one.

RULES OF INVESTING

Many people ask me about the disciplines of investing – the golden rules to making sure you not only make money but also protect what you have already got. It really isn't hard, much of it is simply common sense. The key is discipline.

So here are my golden rules of investing. They are not hard and fast laws but if you don't already have your own 'rules' they may help you establish some personal guidelines.

- **If you can afford it own your own home.** It is the only item exempt from capital gains tax, and can provide a solid base from which you can launch into other investments.

- **Pay off all your debts.** Most investment advisers will start from this piece of advice. If you have spare cash lying around, it is far better to get even with the creditors than to invest elsewhere. After all, there is no use earning 5 per cent on your investment when the bank is taking 16 per cent on your bankcard or Mastercard. One rule of thumb says debts should be no more than 15 per cent of take-home pay (excluding house repayments) before you embark on an investment program.

- **Don't invest until you have adequate insurance.** You should have adequate cover of term-life and disability insurance as well as on your house and car. How much is enough will depend on your circumstances.

- **Limit yourself to investing 10 per cent of investment in risky projects.** This may sound dangerous but we all know that without risk there is no return, so a sensible amount of a portfolio should be in some area of risk to ensure you get some above-average returns. But make sure you do your homework first and get good advice from a sharebroker or financial planner.

- **When you get advice, consider the source of the information.** This is important because advice can be coloured by an individual's personal preferences. Stockbrokers will recommend the sharemarket and funds managers will lean towards managed funds, so try to find an independent adviser who doesn't have a barrow to push. Even then, get a second or third opinion. (We'll return to this subject a little later.)
- **Try to invest 15 per cent of after-tax income.** This is not easy but it is worth striving for. If you don't set a savings goal you may never get ahead.
- **Keep three months' income in a savings account.** There is no point having money in any see-sawing investment if you don't have savings for everyday living. If too much money is tied up in investments you could be tempted to sell investments at the wrong time, for the sake of convenience.
- **Keep another six months' income in a secure fixed-interest account.** This is for the same reason as above but you will receive better interest on the money and provide an even steadier base for risky investments.
- **Diversify your holdings.** This could very well be *the* golden rule of investing, but is particularly relevant to the sharemarket. A broad exposure to all investment possibilities allows you to weather any falls. If one share or asset class crashes, you only have a portion of your portfolio in there and

should be insulated by the rest. Simply put, it's the 'Don't put all your eggs in the one basket' story.

- **If buying into the stockmarket, buy shares when they are undervalued.** This way, hopefully, the only way is up. One way to find the right time to buy is to examine their price-to-earnings ratio. An average PE ratio is ten to fifteen times the earnings per share.
- **Hold shares for the long term.** The stockmarket is a proven performer over long periods but in the short term it can be volatile. Also, frequent trading can mean paying a lot in brokerage fees.
- **Tread lightly around gold, silver and collectibles.** These are fine as a small part of an overall investment scheme. They are nice to look at but value is often subjective and volatile.
- **Tax shelters should be considered as investments first and tax dodges second.** Try to see beyond the veneer of tax returns and look at investment returns. Bizarre tax schemes involving anything from salmon to pecan nuts are just asking for trouble.
- **Use borrowed money sparingly.** It may be true that you can maximise capital gains, but on the flipside, losses will also hit hard. Negative gearing is a lost cause for most people in a low-inflation/low-interest rate environment. Study it carefully.
- **If buying into managed funds, look for consistent returns.** Often managed funds can have a good year and the results look astounding, but dig

deeper. The fund may be top heavy in volatile investments, so while one year it may be great, the next it could fall through the floor. Examine the track record for the last five to ten years (minimum) to make sure the good year's results weren't a fluke.

- **If corporate bonds are your preference, buy only high quality.** Bond issues from a somewhat shaky organisation may have high yields, but if you want to speculate, do it in the stockmarket. Also, consider your tax bracket when buying bonds or deciding whether to cash them in. There may be advantages in getting out before maturation if you are in a low tax bracket.

- **Steer clear of short selling, options trading and commodities speculation.** These really are for the experts. You don't only need to know what's going up and coming down (which is hard enough), but you need to know when it's moving.

- **Don't ignore superannuation.** Super is a great way of saving for retirement and the government is doing its best to make it tax-effective. Well worth a look.

FINDING THE BEST ADVICE

Investing our money is one of the most important things we do. We work hard for it and if we do it reasonably well, we have more than a fair chance of being financially independent in our later years.

But do we give it our best shot? Do we give enough serious thought to what we want to achieve with our investments, how much money we should put aside and what we should do with it? Do we feel competent to make investment decisions in the light of all the changes in government regulation and the tidal wave of new investments?

The answer to these questions is probably no. Part of the answer is to seek competent, professional investment advice. The other part is to make a commitment to do a little more investment homework yourself. Here's a quick quiz to see whether you need investment help:

- Can you read and comprehend a prospectus?
- Do you know what 'ramping' is?
- Are you likely to be aware of the full implications of your investment decisions?
- Do you know where the 'smart money' is being invested?

If you can't answer these questions, comfortably and honestly, then you do need an investment adviser. Here are some guidelines to help you choose a financial planner.

Where to look
You can seek investment advice from banks, financial planning firms, stockbrokers, insurance companies, accountants and solicitors. Many people go to their banks for advice, and there is nothing wrong with this. But firstly, remember all banks offer their own investment products so you can't expect them to recommend their competition too often. Secondly, banks tend to have links with insurance and funds management arms of their own but they cannot guarantee investments in these areas like they can with savings

deposits. One of the implications of this is that the absolute safety and guarantee of your money deposited with the bank does not carry through to other products they offer.

The big names in the investment advice business are established exclusively to advise on investments. They generally have competent and well-trained professional staff. It is common in these organisations for a senior executive to check each individual recommended portfolio before it is submitted to the investor. These companies either have their own research department or purchase the research from specialist organisations. They also often conduct free seminars to attract new clients.

The big stockbrokers frequently have financial planning arms. Such groups seek business from the general public and don't just focus on sharemarket investors.

Insurance companies concentrate on marketing their own products, mainly through their network of insurance agents.

Independent financial planners are people who have chosen to work for themselves. They may be accountants or ex-bankers or have previously worked for a larger advisory firm. Many provide a good service and, because they are small operations, you will get personal attention from the expert.

Credentials

All people giving investment advice today must be licensed by the Australian Securities and Investments Commission, either individually or through the

company that employs them. When checking creden-
tials, ask the following:

- Are they a member of the Financial Planning
  Association (FPA), the professional adviser asso-
  ciation in Australia?
- How old is the company?
- Are there references available from existing
  clients?
- What other businesses are operated by the
  company? Are there any conflicts of interest,
  such as a formal link with a funds manager or an
  insurance company?
- What is the adviser's professional background?
- Does the company have any supporting facilities,
  such as tax specialists, on staff?
- Is there any indemnity insurance?

The cost of advice

You may pay a fee to the adviser who rebates all commissions earned on the products back to you, or the
adviser may be paid commission from the products in
which you invest. Bear in mind that the cheapest fee
is not always the best. Commissions must be fully dis-
closed to you, and you can form your own opinion on
the integrity of the advice.

See at least two advisers before making a
decision, but don't try to see too many or you'll be
confused. Here's a list of what you can expect from a
financial adviser:

- Regular access to information concerning investment markets and topics such as tax.
- A written report of your recommended portfolio.

- Proof that the investment action has been taken. Ask for the original certificates, and let the adviser keep the photocopies; but remember to keep the certificates in a secure place.
- Access to the adviser, either by phone or personally, if you get nervous about your investments at any time.
- Reports on the progress of your investments, along with comments on the investment environment generally.

The first interview

The first interview is probably the most important move into the investment world. Be well prepared before you go to a financial planner. Write down such information as the amount of money you have to invest; details of other income received; financial assets; family details; family budget of income and expenses; any unusually large items of spending planned; and possible lifestyle changes. If you are married, take your partner along. You'll feel less inhibited about asking questions and less ignorant.

Pick an adviser with whom you feel relaxed, one who makes you feel at ease. The best advisers will always be able to do this. They'll generate a professional but relaxed atmosphere in the interview. Take along written notes and questions you want specifically answered.

Ask about costs and payments before employing the adviser. The adviser will disclose what commissions are to be paid on investments recommended. Use your judgment to determine whether this has influenced their advice.

Beware of possible bias

If an adviser tells you to put all your eggs in one basket then it's likely they have a vested interest in your doing so. Generally, advisers will tell you to diversify investments.

One common problem is that you may have to wait several years for results to emerge before knowing whether you have a good adviser or not. 'Growth' investment strategies are generally geared to the medium term (three to five years) or to the long term (five years plus).

Don't let an adviser bombard you with jargon or gibberish. If you don't understand anything have it repeated in terms you understand – that's what you're paying the adviser for. If you still don't understand what they're talking about, they are not for you, so go and find another.

Seminars are worth attending. They give an opportunity to compare advisers and advice, and learn at the same time.

On the topic of safety, the higher the return, the higher the risk. When you're younger you might be better off taking some risk instead of erring on the side of caution. But if you are approaching retirement, then safety first is the name of the game. Make sure you don't exceed the level of risk that you are comfortable with.

RULES FOR PERSONAL INVESTING

Forget about investing in an ad hoc way; the key is to develop your own personal set of rules. But, at the same time, remember that investing is not a science; every individual has different needs.

Before investing, it is important to make a commitment to stick to whatever you decide. These rules should be specifically tailored to your lifestyle and involve guidelines and techniques that you are comfortable with. Due to the natural volatility of investments, decisions will change in line with shifts in the economy and markets, but your basic investment strategy should stand firm and weather these storms. Only drastic changes in income or lifestyle should see you falter.

In fact, it can be harmful to shift your basic investment policy. Look at it this way: it's like changing queues in a supermarket. The other queue always looks faster but once you switch, someone inevitably has an unmarked item that requires a price check.

Making money takes time and is a combination of persistence and patience. This is not to say that you should stubbornly defy change. Few rules and regulations are likely to remain in exactly the same form; it is the basic principles that should be firm.

A stable platform of needs may be served by altering a strategy slightly, but only once you are sure that the old guidelines are no longer relevant. Most importantly, make this decision with care and consideration. Your best friend will be a good sharebroker or financial planner with whom you keep in close contact. But this does not release you from a personal commitment to set your own guidelines and responsibilities.

There are some dos and don'ts that are generally applicable to all investors and can be adapted to an individual case when selecting an investment:

• Investigate an investment from head to toe. Never

buy or sell on impulse, rumour or that intangible quality called a hunch. Very few of us are tuned into our sixth sense enough to put money on it.

- Don't drop the investigation after you have put money into an investment either. There is no such thing as 'set and forget' in the finance world.
- A half-yearly review of the investments should be undertaken to determine whether to hold or sell. You may need to check your investments even more regularly, depending on market forces.
- Bear in mind that all investments come with risks, so equate the risks with the rewards.
- As a rule of thumb, avoid any investment that does not offer twice as much chance of rising as it does of sinking like a brick.

The amount of risk to take will vary. For example, a retiree may choose to invest safely and back a sturdy company, despite lower returns. As Derryn Hinch once said: 'Expect the unexpected.' He could easily have been talking about the stockmarket.

Due to the vast numbers of stocks available, it is best to specialise in one area rather than become a jack of all stocks and a master of none. Keep a prospective investment list small and selective, and try to be intimate with them all. Spreading yourself too thin will increase the margin for error, as your judgment cannot be as well informed. There is no set number of investments to hold but be able to gauge how many you can handle.

At the risk of nagging, *be patient*. Do not change shares like your underwear because it will only cut potential profits and put your stockbroker's children through private school. Unless you are very lucky or know something someone else doesn't (which is very illegal), profit will not increase sufficiently to justify any frenzied changes. Furthermore, this will see you stray from the investment rules. There are few occasions that actually warrant breaking your own rules.

Even if it seems that an investment opportunity requires a deviation, bear in mind that there are hundreds of investments to choose from. Another less damaging opportunity is bound to surface.

So be true to the fences you've erected and run a share portfolio within your own boundaries. With any luck it won't stray too far from home.

Remember your age

When planning an investment strategy, age should be one of the first things you think about. When you are young, it will pay to have a sensible approach to the future, but it is a bit ridiculous tying up every cent in planning for the future and not having any fun. Moderation and common sense are important too.

If you are 20 years old or less, concentrate on developing a savings strategy and not letting all that hard-earned money from your first job slip through your fingers. Even $10 or $20 a week is a good start. From the age of 20 to 30, you are laying the foundation for a work life and, more often than not, getting married and planning a family. Quite often during this time you have two incomes. Make the most of it, and if a home is a priority, take advantage of the second income to make some inroads into the repayments.

> Extra money paid off on a home loan saves thousands of dollars of future interest.
>
> After your thirties and throughout your forties you'll find the children are usually at their most expensive. But now is the time to start thinking seriously about the future and planning for retirement. You have at least twenty years to put in place a sensible strategy.
>
> Once you are in your fifties, you will probably find yourself more financially independent than you've ever been. All those good habits of the past will pay off, and you have at this stage of your life the greatest opportunity to create wealth.
>
> Until the grandchildren come along.

THE PORTFOLIO APPROACH

To David's immensely practical advice, I would add one 'big picture' concern. We have already discussed the subject of career planning in detail in Chapter 7, but when considering family finances, diversification of income streams is as important in a modern career as it is in an investment portfolio.

Increasingly, work over our lifetimes will be less a series of single jobs with companies and more a series of jobs and roles across different organisations, and increasingly across different – but related – skill sets. Employers are growing more and more reluctant to enter into expensive employment contracts when they can outsource much of their work and access the flexible external skill base offered by contractors.

For the individual, this might seem a scary alternative to the 'job for life', but whether it is frightening or not, it is the way the workplace is moving. It does, however, provide you with an opportunity to actively pursue a career that might be more satisfying than the one you are concentrating on at the moment: the cool term now is 'micro-business'. It provides the chance to develop a broader range of skills and create ongoing personal development opportunities, while at the same time allowing for income diversification.

Creating a micro-business

You have limited resources, financial and time-wise. The goal is to try to develop income streams that will take the pressure off your main work role. This not only provides potentially more income, but also job security unrelated to your core job.

It goes without saying that it is difficult to develop a micro-business if you are working 60 hours a week, so the main issue might be how to cut down on your main work time, to allow time to think about and manage a developing income stream.

GREG'S FITNESS BUSINESS

Greg worked long hours in a middle management role in a large industrial company. But he had a great interest in health and fitness, and began developing a personal training regimen.

Initially he secured two clients for his new fitness program. It meant he had to get up early two days a week to service his clients, and meet them after work twice a week. Over time, he picked up a couple more clients, to the point where his fitness work, the part of his working day that he enjoyed most, began to seriously cut into his job time.

Greg's problems with working long hours weren't lost on his employers, but Greg took charge of the situation – he noticed that his organisation was using temporary consulting services and pitched himself into one of the roles. He now works part time as a consultant at his company, and part time as a fitness trainer. He has a strong client list, and even though the work isn't as lucrative as his day job, he enjoys it much more.

He tells me that he is more fulfilled, feels like he has more control over his destiny, and that he has cut the umbilical cord to the big company and the big organisation. Of course this 'umbilical cord' had never really existed. But it was real enough in Greg's mind, as he'd been relying on it for many years to provide him with self-esteem and a role in life. His 'micro-business' has helped him overcome that perception and live a more balanced life.

IT'S ALRIGHT FOR YOU, TOO

'Financial independence' is a relative term. In a recent survey, the majority of Australians said that if they were to achieve an income of A$100 000 a year, they would consider themselves rich. For others, that figure might be much more, or much less. I have friends who earn less than $100 000 a year and through careful expense planning and investment consider themselves to have financial stability and be on the road to financial independence. But I know of others who earn multiples of $100 000 per year and are struggling to keep up with their commitments. The point is that a sufficient income will be defined according to your own needs, and how those needs are to be fulfilled.

The important and yet difficult decision is determining how much income you really need to be able to establish an acceptable level of financial independence. This in turn requires an honest evaluation of the motivation for buying 'things', which in itself is a difficult process for some because it brings into focus some of the insecurities we all carry.

Wherever you are on the income pyramid, it is essential to understand the financial basis of your life if you are to build the platform for a well-balanced and an absolutely (as opposed to relatively) successful future. Beyond an obvious base level, it is not about the amount of money you have, but the life you truly aspire to live.

Two other important legs on the stool are health and relationships, which we shall look at in the next chapter, 'Body and soul'.

09

BODY AND SOUL

I am often amazed at the way seemingly intelligent people treat their health. They work long hours, take little exercise, eat garbage, drink to excess and often smoke. It seems a bit pointless to spend most of your life in an office, stoking up your blood pressure and destroying your body in order to get rich, while the probability of being alive to enjoy the fruits of your labour is rapidly dwindling. Dying prematurely is something that only happens to other people – until it happens to you.

Equally, there is little point in expending the emotional and intellectual effort on developing a balanced life if you are not going to be around to enjoy the relationships that you have developed and the life you've nurtured. The reality is that if you want to increase your chances of living past 80 years of age in good health, you need to have a health and fitness regimen that focuses on keeping your body healthy. More than that, a healthy body and a healthy mind go hand in hand. People who are fit and eat well perform much better in the workplace. They are sharper, have more energy, and are less prone to illness.

Look at two types of assets a business may have. On the one hand it may have a piece of equipment (such as a printing press for a printing company) that cost $2 million. The business will also have employees – let's say that one of them earns $100 000 a year. Taking this income level you could generate an argument that the employee has an asset value to the business of between $1 million and $4 million, depending on your view on asset yields.

It is highly likely that the $2 million printing press needs regular maintenance and repairs, and that its use is carefully planned so that it can deliver long term perform-ance for the company. On the other hand, in all likelihood, there is no such asset maintenance for the $4 million employee. Two assets, both valuable, and yet there are two completely different approaches to them.

While some companies are starting to assist employees in understanding their health, I still find it remarkable that intelligent, analytical executives spend inor-dinate amounts of time on their company's assets planning while they eat and drink too much, smoke, undertake little exercise, and generally kill themselves, slowly but surely.

It's almost as if, with the working hours we keep and the pressures placed on us, we have to factor in a time to be ill.

We all know the syndrome. You work ridiculous hours before taking a holiday and the moment you're on leave you get sick. Coincidence? No. The body has an amazing ability to pump out adrenaline to keep you performance-focused but when the pressure comes off, your system then realises it can let go, and you fall over sick. The lesson is that you can't work at maximum pace for more than a short period of time, and if you do you, will pay the price through not only short-term sickness but long-term health problems.

I am neither a fitness guru nor a nutritionist, but I have recognised the need to understand these subjects because I can't see the point of putting all the effort into developing a balanced life and actively living it if I am inhibited by bad health or destined for an early death. So I asked David Graham, managing director of health and fitness company Mozsports, who *is* a health, fitness and diet guru, and this is his advice for those starting out on a fitness program.

THE DAVID GRAHAM HEALTH PROGRAM

1. Take the long view

Take some time out to think about where you want to be in ten or twenty years time, in terms of your life. What sort of lifestyle do you want? Are you really keen on learning first-hand about adult-onset diabetes, heart disease, lung cancer, etc? If so, continue with your current regimen. If, however, you want to be active and in good health in your later years, you need to understand that such an outcome takes focus, energy and time. Establish a clear vision of how you want to feel and look in ten years' time, and commit to working towards this vision. (And I'm not talking about Botox schedules but a deeper sense of health and well-being.)

2. Be realistic

Be realistic with your personal goals and objectives when beginning any exercise program. Clarify exactly what you are trying to achieve with each session. By failing to plan, you plan to fail. It may take you as much time to return to good physical condition as it took to achieve your current state of fitness. Have you been slobbing around the office for ten years? Prepare to work slowly, and remain committed. Verbalise your goals to friends and work colleagues – it will only strengthen your commitment.

3. Get a check-up

If you are over 35 years of age, have been sedentary for more than one year or are rehabilitating from an injury, consult your GP before starting any exercise program. Have a full medically supervised health screening at least every two years. Have your blood pressure, body fat skin folds, girth measurements and cholesterol levels taken quarterly, to monitor your progress and give yourself a target to hit. Remember: if you don't have time for your health now, you'll need to find time to be sick later.

4. Time to exercise

Choose an exercise time that fits your lifestyle. Most

choose to exercise early in the day because it is relatively unintrusive on family or work time. Be disciplined with your sleeping hours. If you have trouble getting up early, go to bed an hour earlier. Outsource the procrastination: make a commitment to meet a friend early in the morning. Getting up early is easy if you have the right attitude towards it. (When was the last time you missed the 6.30 am flight to Melbourne because you couldn't get out of bed?)

Lunchtime training sessions are great if time allows. Most CBDs have running or outdoor training groups. Check out your company's corporate health program, and work out with other colleagues.

5. Goal setting

Establish separate short-, mid- and long-term goals. Here's the key: imagine your fitness levels at 30 years of age, again at 40, then 50, 60, and so on. What type of health will you carry into retirement years? Will you have sporting hobbies and interests? Lay the platform now. If the program you're on is working for you, then great, carry on; if not, make changes. Personally I like to start with long-term goals and let the others fall into place. Example: run a marathon before my fortieth birthday.

Keep a yearly fitness planner, similar to your work planner. Schedule health checks, sports events, physical challenges, even fitness holidays (such as trekking, canoeing, skiing) into the plan, just like you would board meetings, birthdays and other work or family commitments.

6. Work and rest

Work through cycles of exercise and rest. Have a cut-off time for each period.

Don't become too obsessed with your program, remember to have some down time for the body to recharge. As a general rule, take one full week off after every twelve weeks of training. Don't become too inflexible with it all. And remember, being extremely fit doesn't necessarily mean you're extremely healthy – health is a holistic function of your lifestyle in its entirety, and implies time for work, rest and play.

7. Select good exercise equipment

A good pair of shoes is a must. The shoe must offer good support, feel comfortable, and be purpose-built for walking, running, gym work or whatever you are doing.

If you are starting a running program, it's a good idea to have an appointment with a sports podiatrist. They can determine which way you run and offer advice on shoes and orthopaedic devices. Have them fitted by a sports-shoe technician. As a rule, the most expensive shoe is not always the best. Socks too are important: get the best pair you can. They should be made of soft, absorbent cotton and elasticised for comfort.

8. Monitor your progress

This can be done in many ways. The most effective way to monitor your workouts is with a personal heart rate monitor. This allows you to (a) check your heart rate while exercising and (b) recall the session to check progress. There are various software programs on the market that track training sessions and chart your progress. It's no different from checking your share portfolio.

9. FITT
Start slowly. Adopt the FITT principle: frequency, intensity, time and type. This is woth explaining in some detail, after which we'll return to steps 10 and 11 of the health program.

Frequency
This is how often you exercise. Consistency is key. When you start a program, aim for three sessions a week; another way to look at it is four days of no exercise. Even if you start with 20 minutes of walking three times a week you will immediately get the benefits of exercise.

Intensity
When you start a cardiovascular program, aim to train at 65 to 80 per cent of maximum heart rate for at least 20 to 30 minutes. Too much too soon will stress the heart. This is where a personal heart rate monitor is convenient. The better models on the market today allow you to program in personal stats, such as age and weight etc, and can calculate percentage heart rates for you. All you need to do is follow your heart rate. If you're not working hard enough, the watch will tell you, just like a personal trainer.

Time
If you have an hour allocated, go for:

- 5 minutes warm-up and stretch
- 20 minutes cardio
- 20 minutes resistance
- 10 minutes fit ball/abs/Pilates
- 5 minutes stretch.

Remember, wait till the engine is fully warm before you hit top speed. If you haven't exercised in a year or more, then I would recommend only brisk walking three times a week for the first month. This will allow your heart and lungs to become conditioned to exercise. As a general rule, your program should increase by 10 per cent each week.

Type
Try to include the following into your program:
- **Resistance or weight training.** Excellent for muscle and bone strength. We achieve our maximum strength around the age of 30; therefore, as we get older, the need for resistance training only increases. Have a personal trainer or gym instructor create a program for you.

  It is a common misconception that muscle turns to fat when you stop training. Muscle and fat are two separate things. You gain weight because you stop burning calories, not because you have too much muscle. When you start a weights program you may encounter a little muscle soreness (or a lot!), depending on how much you lift. DOMS or delayed onset of muscular soreness – usually occurs 24 to 36 hours after vigorous exercise, and is thought to be caused by microscopic tearing of muscles. This is normal, not a sign of weakness, but can be minimised by properly warming up and cooling down before exercising rigorously.

- **Stretching.** Stretching before and after exercise improves the flexibility or extensibility of muscles and tendons. Stretching helps reduce muscle tension, promotes circulation and improves range of motion. And it feels good. Stretching can be performed daily.
- **Cardiovascular or aerobic fitness.** Running, cycling, swimming, kayaking, rowing, trekking and cross-country skiing are all examples of aerobics fitness. Many of these sports can be performed indoors at the gym on stationary equipment.
- **Core stability.** The best way to train is to use the Swiss Balls. Don't be fooled by their poncy appearance: these balls are proving to be one of the best fitness tools to hit the market in the last ten years. They allow the body to work three-dimensionally, unlike stationary weights equipment. Most sports, like golf, tennis and kayaking, use all three dimensions so it's important to exercise through its full range of motion. Balls are excellent for abdominal balance and stability work.
- **Yoga.** Yoga is great for your spiritual fitness, excellent for recharging the batteries. Find a qualified instructor to explain the different forms of yoga and all its benefits.
- **Pilates.** Excellent for working the body inside out. Develops great core strength and control. Again, seek out a qualified teacher to guide you through a workable routine.

- **Massage.** One of the best ways to relax and recover. Massage increases circulation and helps with digestion and removal of lactic acid build-up in the body. Aim to have one a month.

10. Engage others

Seek out others with similar goals and objectives. A support group is essential to keep you going through those low periods that every beginner experiences. These groups can range from work colleagues, old sporting or school friends and touch football groups, to a personal trainer or group training instructor.

11. Basic eating guidelines

- Drink more water – at least 2 litres a day.
- Don't diet. It only serves to make you fatter.
- Cut out sugar from the diet.
- Record and monitor your eating habits for a full week. You will be amazed how conscious you will become of your eating habits. Take your food diary to a dietician.
- Avoid an overload of caffeine. Drinks such as coffee, tea and Red Bull have vast amounts of caffeine. Caffeine is a diuretic, which only serves to dehydrate the body.
- Choose low-GI (Glycaemic Index) foods over high-GI foods.
- Eat plenty of protein, as it's great for recovery and muscle building. If you struggle to find protein foods you enjoy, take a whey protein each morning.
- Reduce the amount of bad fat foods in your diet.

> Not all fats are bad, so it's important to under-
> stand the difference.
> • Eat plenty of fruit and vegetables.

If you do all of the above, you will have done your best to ensure that you have the physical resources to live a long and health life. Physical health alone, however, does not bring about a happy and fulfilled life. To achieve this we need deep relationships with other human beings.

RELATIONSHIPS: FOOD FOR THE SOUL

Without the existence of relationships that touch our hearts and give us a sense of purpose, life is empty and sad. With strong, deep relationships we are less stressed, more energised, feel more valued and live happier and longer lives. Relationships are truly like flowers in the garden. Without attention and suste-nance they will die, and when they are dead, they are dead forever.

It happens so often, the story is now a cliche. The career-focused executive marries in his twenties and ignores his wife and children through his thirties. He wakes up in his forties and accuses his wife of failing to 'grow' with him. His wife meanwhile has spent her life building his home, raising his children and creating the facade of a perfect home life, the suc-cessful family, the spotless and stylish house. He throws money at her in lieu of his time, attention and love. She wonders where the man she married has gone, and in frustration spends the money he has been throwing at her: clothes, lunches, lifestyle. They have, in fact, grown apart.

Divorce and separation ensue. He picks up with a younger woman and, perhaps having learned his lesson, devotes the time and attention to her that he failed to give wife number one.

Or perhaps they never divorce, but when he retires, he comes home to find his wife is not there with him, even if she is still there with him. His kids? Strangers. He is in shock.

Often these men, when they are in their mid-fifties, suddenly find a passion for hanging out with their kids – now teenagers or young adults. The kids have no idea who this middle-aged man is, but they do know that if they spend time with him, all sorts of cool *material* stuff seems to come with the territory: money, ski trips, a car . . . He has no friends to support him in his midlife crisis, and is trying to make up for all that lost time.

Our working careers are so transient, and can in the end be so meaningless. It is difficult to understand why so many of us devote so much time to getting our work careers right, or even to our health and fitness regimen, and so little time to nurturing the only parts of our lives that can give us true significance: our relationships with our loved ones.

According to Relationships Australia, people in supportive, loving relationships are more likely to feel healthier, happier and satisfied with their lives and are less likely to have mental or physical health problems or to do things that are bad for their health. People in this type of relationship help each other practically as well as emotionally. Supportive partners share the good times and help each other through the tough ones.

Breaking up can be a health hazard, but that doesn't make it any less common:

- One in three first marriages end in divorce, two in three second marriages end in divorce.
- Most people who get divorced have been married less than ten years.
- People aged 23 to 30 are in the highest risk group for relationship problems and breakdown.

It usually takes two to three years for a couple whose relationship has broken up to begin to put their lives back together again. It sometimes takes five years for individuals and families to get over the emotional pain and trauma. Many people can have serious health and emotional problems during this time. Many men, women and children sink into poverty after a separation and are forced to rely on welfare benefits to survive. Their standard of living drops dramatically.

And in the end, many people wish they hadn't split up. Again, according to Relationships Australia, 37 per cent of people regret their divorce five years later, while up to 40 per cent of divorced people believe their divorce could have been avoided.

But relationships, like anything else in life, are manageable if you put the right kind of thought and effort into them. If we were to put as much energy into developing our relationships as we do our business plans or political strategies, we would be surrounded by supportive and loving people.

Take a moment to think about your key relationships:

- Parents
- Siblings
- Aunts, uncles, cousins (we'll call these the 'add-ons')
- Spouse/partner
- Children
- Friends.

Having thought about some of these, you may decide that to let one or two of these relationships die would not be a great tragedy. In some cases you may not want to develop your relationship with your parents, aunts and uncles or cousins. That is of course your choice – just make sure you are clear why you are choosing to let this particular relationship die, and do so in the knowledge that once gone it can't be re-created.

Others, however, you will value greatly. Like anything of value in life, you will need to work at them, allocating time, energy and focus. I am amazed that men who neglect their wives or children for ten to fifteen years can then be in shock when their wives walk out on them or their children do not want to spend time with them.

In simple terms, in order to develop stronger relationships with those who are close to you, you need to choose to do so, and allocate time to this.

We live incredibly busy lives. The demands of the workplace and home and family lives are non-stop and exhausting. According to several recent surveys, many Australians are suffering under the burden of the demands on their lives. A Relationships Australia survey published early in 2004 revealed that while nine out of ten people think that family is more important than work, that same figure believe that their main relationships are falling apart because of work commitments:

- 89% said that relationships were in trouble because balancing work and life was so difficult.
- 100% believe that being a good parent is important.
- 99% believe that being a good partner is important.
- 83% said that having a paid job is important.
- 24% of people in full-time employment would like to change their work patterns.
- 40% of parents felt they had no real choices.
- 38% of couples said that lack of time together harmed their relationship.

'We seem to have a gambling mentality towards relationships – people leave them to chance and hope for the best,' Anne Hollonds, chief executive of Relationships Australia NSW, told the *Sun-Herald*.

But the key to successfully finding the balance between work and home life is not to gamble but to make decisions. Melinda Mulroney, mother of two young girls, was also interviewed by the *Sun-Herald*: 'It all comes down to making deliberate choices between career and family.' Melinda works as a corporate lawyer, rather than in a partnership, because it gives her more time flexibility, while her husband pursues his career as a chartered boat skipper around time spent caring for the children. 'It means there is not much time left,' she admitted. 'Time is my enemy.'

These are the relationship challenges we all face. I am concerned that too many people face these challenges unconsciously, without actively deciding on how they will surmount them. To repeat, the key to finding a balance is to *deliberately* make choices.

SUCCESS IN THE WORKPLACE

The ironic thing is that according to much of the academic work done in this area, sacrificing a home life for the sake of work does you no good whatsoever in the workplace. One study by Peter Cappelli, Jill Constantine and Clint Chadwick at the Wharton School, University of Pennsylvania, published as 'It pays to value family: Work and family trade-offs reconsidered', found that a determination to have a happy family life was the most important factor in life earnings.

The researchers, led by the co-director of the school's centre for human resources, analysed a survey of people who were in their last year of high school in 1972 and tracked their progress through to 1986, when a second survey was carried out. The study compared their work-oriented personal priorities while at school, such as 'success in work', 'having money' and 'finding steady work', with their later success in terms of their salaries.

The study found that the only major link between attitude and income later in life was among men who emphasised 'finding the right person to marry and having a happy family life'. The only other trait in the high school students that seemed to have an impact on later income was 'having strong friendships', and that only slightly. Having a family at some point, even if they were no longer with the family at the time of the later survey, also had a positive effect on income.

The academics at the Wharton School tentatively concluded that we hold wrong assumptions: we assume that having a family life detracts from our ability to focus on work, but this is wrong. Having a family gives people balance and focus, and these people make better employees. More than this, having a bad family life makes even greater demands on a person's time and attention: 'consider how bad marriages, divorce and other family conflicts disrupt one's overall life. These problems make different kinds of demands on individuals than the requirements of a good family'. The moral could almost be: If you can't make time for your marriage now, you'll have to make time for your divorce later.

GIVING BACK

Earlier in the book, I referred to Erik Erikson's psychological model and how in your later years, he would argue, we tend to think more about the needs of others and society as a whole. It's part of the balance, the enrichment of body and soul.

Personally I have noticed that I tend to get enormous joy from being involved in community activities. It is not the size of the commitment that matters but rather the simple fact that you are doing something for someone else with no thought of the 'return on investment' or what you will get out of it. Currently I am involved in a full range of community activities, from assisting on the school board through to coaching sports teams and donating funds to a range of worthy causes (through our family foundation).

Let's briefly look at the concept of giving back, starting with the big end of town.

Bill Gates' approach to philanthropy is one that should be modelled by all wealthy Australians. The Bill and Melinda Gates Foundation (run by Bill, his father, and his wife) currently has an endowment of US$26 billion, most of which is to be dedicated to solving health and education problems in the developing world. By the time he dies, more than 95 per cent of his entire fortune will be in the foundation.

Bill's father was a wealthy Seattle solicitor, and his mother was a very committed philanthropist. For Mary Gates, community giving was not just a choice – it was what you do when you have been fortunate enough to do well. She was a committed philanthropist and on the board of many of Seattle's charitable organisations. For Bill then, philanthropy was also a duty.

Over the years I have had a few discussions with Bill Gates about philanthropy. While the formal process only started a few years ago he had been thinking about philanthropy for many years. Bill's charity started tentatively, focusing mostly on donating computers to libraries and schools around Seattle, before he started to look internationally. But on a visit in the early '90s to the black township of Soweto near Johannesburg, Bill saw that these poor communities have little use for computers plugged into fitful generators. And reading about millions dying from preventable diseases in the 1993

World Development Report convinced him that his money could best be spent in the developing world. Recent grants from the foundation have included US$89.2 million to develop new tuberculosis vaccines and US$168 million to fight malaria in Africa.

Since setting up the foundation, Bill has focused his laser-like intelligence on his giving activities, devoting as much drive and insight into his philanthropy as he does his business activities. He is extremely fussy about where the money goes, and is just as concerned about waste and ineffi-ciency in charitable and community activity as at Microsoft. In the discussions I've had with Bill, what is most striking is that he sees philanthropy as a responsibility that needs to be exercised with enormous energy and dedication.

When I asked him about donating to causes he made a very valid point: in the USA and Australia there is enough money around to solve the nation's problems, it is just a matter of the society deciding to fix the issues. In parts of Africa and other third-world locations, however, this is not the case. There is not enough money to buy cheap vaccines to stop children dying, nor to provide clean water for local communi-ties. I found these discussions incredibly insightful and while over time Bill has given some money to US charities and causes, the bulk of his philanthropy is directed to poor coun-tries and seemingly intractable problems.

The poverty of wealth in Australia

In truth, while the average Australian is relatively philan-thropic – giving generous donations to charity – the country's wealthy are appallingly tight-fisted. With few exceptions (Myer Family is one), the majority of very wealthy Australians allocate less than 10 per cent of their wealth to philanthropy and *much* less than 10 per cent of their time and energy to philanthropic causes. The average Australian (pro rata) donates similar amounts to charities as their American counterpart, but there is a big difference when you look at the comparison between wealthy Americans and wealthy Australians.

It appears that while the average Australian has a strong culture of giving back to the community, the rich do not – which is a bit upside down to me. The truly Australian culture of helping each other out, giving the shirt off your back for a mate or neighbour, is alive and well, it seems, for all but wealthy Australians.

It is a mystery to me why this is, and why the newspapers will trumpet an $11 million one-time major commitment from a multi-billionaire. That is like someone who has surplus assets (over and above their house(s) and everything they need for their lifestyle) of, say, $2 million giving $2000 over the course of their lives: most people would consider this an absolutely minimal gesture. Given that the billionaire probably has at least $500 million that he doesn't need – no matter how glitzy his lifestyle – surely he could put this into a foundation that could throw off $50 million a year, every year?

I have discussed this topic with many wealthy Australian business people and the most common response is 'The tax rates are too high, so why should I give?' or, even more common, 'It's *my* money – why should I give it away?'

Tax rates may be higher than in some countries, although as a whole Australia is one of the lower taxing nations within the OECD. But the point is that these people have still ended up with a net worth of $20 million, $50 million, $500 million, $1 billion, or whatever. In absolute terms, they do not need all this money to live on, whatever lifestyle they aspire to.

The other thing I wonder about is, while they may have made money out of some successful or lucky venture, don't they feel even a twinge of guilt when they see advertisements of starving kids in Africa, homeless youths on the streets of Australia, or young people with no access to decent health and education facilities? Without wanting to put too fine a point on it, how do they sleep at night?

Take the *BRW* Top 200 Rich List. The poorest person on the list has about $80 million, and the richest, $5.5 billion. For all of the lucky 200, let's propose a modest tithe to charity of 10 per cent. The guy on Struggle Street with just $80 million would be giving up $8 million – does anyone imagine that they could really miss $8 million given they have $72 million left to live on? Apply the same tithe from top to bottom of the Rich List, and the total endowment for all the foundations would be something between $2 billion and $3 billion – an asset that could provide an annual income of $300 million, which could be invested in needy charities.

An extra $300 million a year being donated to needy charities with no material change in the lives of the donors. It's the closest thing to a free lunch society could have. To be in the top 1 per cent of personal *and* corporate givers in Australia, you need to give away just $200 000 in any one year. Imagine what $300 million could do for our society.

More foundations are being established – about 200 new ones in the last few years. But the harsh reality is that while there has been growth, the sum total of charitable donations in Australia is risible compared to the amounts that we spend on truly worthless consumption. I propose a 10 per cent tithe on the seriously wealthy. If you are worth anything north of $20 million (around 1000 people in Australia), you could easily give up 10 per cent of your net worth without changing your lifestyle one iota. The reward would be the satisfaction of making such a positive contribution to the world in which we live.

While the concept of giving back has not yet resonated with many of the wealthy and powerful members of our society – they have yet to experience the true joy that giving (till it hurts!) can bring – a happy and successful life is predicated on doing just that. I constantly meet people who have in their later years devoted significant time and resources to a variety of worthy causes, and their sense of purpose and fulfilment is palpable. You do not have to be an Australian multi-millionaire to experience this feeling. Allocating a small sum from your income to something you really care about, or, if finances are tight, allocating some time to help a local cause, will bring you rewards that are immeasurable and addictive. Giving back could be as simple as helping with Meals on Wheels, being the person at the school crossing some mornings during the week or helping with a local charity drive. It may just be sponsoring a child overseas or helping out on Clean Up Australia Day or with the Red Cross or Salvation Army appeals.

The key to achieving the true rewards from giving back, it seems to me, is giving away something that matters to you. Therefore, giving money away that you will notice when it is gone actually creates a sense of purpose and joy, as does giving up time for a community activity that you might normally have used to play sport or undertake some other personal pursuit. I am convinced that to lead a truly happy life we must have this dimension of giving back – without it, at some point, our lives will seem empty, greedy and pointless.

HOLISTIC HEALTH

A healthy body, healthy relationships and a sense of giving are an integral part of achieving sustainable success. Nobody is responsible for the health of your body and soul but you, and there are active things that you can do to achieve them. Surely you owe it to yourself and your loved ones to pursue them.

For some years now I have been on the President's Council at the Children's Hospital at Westmead. I gain great fulfilment from adding whatever value I can to this world-class institution but, still, I am often hesitant before I go there. The hospital showcases both extreme sadness, when one sees the illnesses of young children, and incredible joy, in the extraordinary services provided to kids to make them better. I know that by visiting I am going to have an extremely emotionally draining time at the hospital, moving between sadness and joy, and constantly in awe of the wonderful people who work there.

There is a 'realness' about the hospital that puts into perspective other things in my life (such as achieving quarterly revenue targets), and the hospital exposure provides a marker for me to understand how fortunate I am. When I get home after a visit to Westmead, I cannot help reaching out to my family and giving them the mother and father of all hugs. *We are just so lucky to have each other and our health, how could we possibly be unhappy or in any way dissatisfied with our lives?* The hospital provides a reality check, a re-establishment of perspective, a recalibration. For some time after a visit I retain a very clear sense of what really matters to me and am able to fend off the normal human, ego-driven desires to be busy and get more.

I am convinced that those of us who live healthy lives, free of major health or other trauma, lose perspective as to what really matters – the underlying real truth about what makes us happy. We get caught up in an often selfish process of being busy, achieving more, getting more, and constantly looking over our shoulders to see how we are doing compared to our peers. Generally our work promotes these feelings and desires, and left unchecked we become conditioned to thinking that working 60 hours a week is not such a bad thing, that having had two failed marriages is just what happens, that having kids run off the rails is just what kids do, that we really do need that new car, house, suit and all the rest to be happy. Unfortunately, while we all desperately need it, too few of us have a regular reality check.

I also love the people at the hospital. They are so *real*, so confident in what they are doing, so motivated by addressing the needs of others, and so . . . nice. So very different from the environment in which I am used to working, in other words, the cut and thrust and competing egos of the corporate world. The business world could use a major injection of the spirit of Westmead – an understanding that we are extremely fortunate to be able to do what we do and enjoy it, to be healthy and alive, and to have real choices available to us – choices that the children in hospital do not.

Yet again, it comes down to perspective and choice. 'Choices?' I often hear. 'I don't *have* any choices.' All too often when I talk about work–life balance, people tell me that they are *trapped*. They have financial responsibilities. They work at an organisation where the culture demands 'commitment' (read: insane work hours). They can't move jobs just yet, they need to prove themselves a bit more. They are not in the privileged position that I am in, they say – 'It's alright for you.'

While some of this is valid (we all have financial responsibilities and some of us do work for unreasonable organisations), the responses are framed within a context that assumes a particularly work-focused view of life. What annoys me so much about this framework is that it avoids the whole discussion. It throws the light away from the topic of conversation – your life, what it is about, what you want it to be and whether you are happy in it – and implies that the pursuit of happiness, satisfaction and purpose in life can be postponed. These people are saying that they can only be free to take choices and be happy after a particular goal has been attained (after the mortgage is paid off, after they've been promoted to vice-president, after they've bought a new car). In actual fact, it is the goal itself that is preventing them from taking those choices. I often respond with something along the lines of: 'What would you do if tomorrow you found out you had a year to live or that your child or wife was very sick? Would you respond the same way?'

In all cases the respondents recalibrate their *perspective* on the situation and realise that they do in fact have some choices, and would exercise these choices if certain circumstances existed. The key then is to remove the concept of major trauma and try to maintain the same 'whole of life/life is short' perspective.

Life is a complex, multifaceted thing. It is hard for all, and very hard for some. Each part of our lives – work, family, friends, community, our legacy – takes time and attention. If you don't keep your eye on any of these balls you will, sure as eggs, drop them. You only have one life, after all, and to miss out on any one part of it because you simply weren't paying attention is tragic. If you take a rational, conscious choice to forego a particular part of life, then fine. But to lose out purely because of a lack of perspective is quite sad.

Relinquishing responsibility for determining the purpose in your life to your employer might give you someone to blame, but it won't give you your life back. If you have come this far in this book, you know that you have a choice. Now it is up to you to exercise it.

CORPORATE CONDITIONING

'I am happy with my life.' More often than not this comes from the executive who is working 60 hours or more a week, taking a couple of weeks' holiday a year (during which the flu mysteriously strikes), not seeing their kids between Monday morning and Friday night, not having had a meaningful conversation about life with their spouse for years, and not pursuing any real hobbies (other than the corporately required golf game). Like Wayne, the corporate hero we met in the introduction, it generally doesn't take too much probing to determine that in actual fact they are not happy, they are deeply dissatisfied. But they have become conditioned. Conditioned to believe that their work is their life and that this is actually a good thing!

I have come to see those executives who easily fool themselves into thinking they are happy in their overworked lives as victims of corporate conditioning. They simply do not have the perspective to see just how completely messed up their life is. Often it is these people who will need a radical wake-up call, a catalyst to enable them to see things through a more realistic prism. The death of a family member, perhaps, or a child getting sick, or being told they have a life-threatening disease. If you have come this far in this book and are still reading, consider yourself lucky, you may have taken the first step in avoiding a nasty wake-up call!

A HAPPY LIFE

It is a simple but profound truth: a happy life is not built of mortgages, pay rises and promotions. Working longer hours will not necessarily make you more successful, more likely it will do just the opposite. As Eckersley points out in *Well & Good*, happiness is a function of: 'Marriage, religion, friends, leisure, health, money and work . . . personal control, social support, optimism . . . A sense of belonging is important as is a sense of meaning in your life . . .'

Individualism (the mantra of the new millennium) actually does not seem to lead to greater happiness. It may lead to great independence and to the achievement of more specific individual goals, but there is no conclusive evidence to show that a strong individual focus actually produces a happier outcome for the individual.

The answer to the riddle of how to have a happy life is to listen to your inner voice and allow yourself to live the life you truly want to lead, and not the life you have been told you should lead. This voice will talk about love, belonging, care, communication, safety, support, development and contentment.

It takes strength to focus on feelings and the intangible yet ultimately more sustaining notions of care, belongingness and love. It is not easy. It takes inner strength to look at people who have 'more' than you and not feel inadequate; to understand that a successful life is more than simply financial success; to understand that some people may be financially successful but spectacularly unsuccessful in other parts of their lives. If it's role models you need, choose to search for *complete* people.

As a leader – of a corporation, a government organisation, a small business, a sporting team or a home – you have a responsibility to ensure the environment you create is better for your being there. Your behaviour needs to have a positive impact on the lives of others and you need to be a positive role model for those who have yet to work out the costs of trade-offs in life. This is not something a leader can opt out of. It comes with the territory. A CEO of one company I work for says that he does not care about employee morale, all he cares about are the numbers. His view is that if the numbers are okay, people will get paid, and that is all people care about. This CEO, like so many others we've come across in these pages, is clearly out of step with a major change sweeping through our society.

Just as the polls are telling us that we do not want more tax cuts (individual benefit) but would rather the money be put into schools, hospitals and services, we are seeing that people want more out of life than just more money and more possessions.

CLOSING EXERCISES

As stated in the introduction, this book is intended to be a practical one. In this final section, I have included some tips to help you make a change in your life. All change is scary, but the key to changing anything, from the organisation that you lead through to the life you live, is to take small steps first, to collect the low hanging fruit, and to have a clear vision of where you are going to.

Stopping the world

- Every week or so take some time in the evening to sit quietly by yourself in a room, with no distractions or interruptions, and think about your life and where is it going. Allow your mind to wander through all parts of your life but do not dwell on work. Think about your health, your relationships, your interests.

- During this same session, ask yourself, 'What do I need to be really happy?' Think this through and test your responses. If you initially think that a salary increase of $10 000 will make you really happy, think this through. It might or it might not. The key is not what I or anyone else might think – what matters is what *you* really think.

Keeping perspective

Every now and then visit your local children's hospital or aged persons' facility. See the wonderful work that's done there and look at how families are coping with illnesses and issues with their children. Then ask yourself three things:

1. Do I appreciate what I have? 2. Is my life heading down a track that I'm happy with? 3. Am I doing enough to provide support for those in need?

- Don't read the papers or watch the TV news for a week. See that the world actually keeps going and your life does not grind to a halt without the daily selected dosage of murder and mayhem that many media outlets feel it is their duty to dump on us.
- Once a year take a day off work and take your kids out of school (with appropriate permissions of course!) for a special non-school-holiday day out. Visit a park, have picnic, go for a surf.

  Come home early from work once or twice a month and just hang around the kids and your spouse (who may have to come home work early as well!), and become part of the afternoon ritual. See how much more engaged the kids are in the afternoon.

Use this experience to help you focus on efficiency next time you're in the office at 5.30 pm and just about to start a new piece of work as opposed to going home.

- Visit someone much older than you and ask them about their life and their perspective on what life is about. Ask them for their advice on how to live a happy and fulfilled life.

Making time

- Take ownership of your diary. It is yours after all. *You* decide what meetings or other activities get put in there.
- Only attend meetings where a decision is going to be made. Updates can be more efficiently provided through emails.
- Don't start meetings before 9 am or after 4.30 pm. That way you might have a chance to take your kids to school or be home for dinner every now and then.
- At the beginning of the year, diarise all major events – birthday dinners, anniversary dinners, school concerts, parent–teacher nights, sports events, special days off, and then keep those dates. Write in your exercise times, and make time for other interests and to develop your relationships. Now you can fit the rest of your work life around the important events in your life.
- Don't get caught up in other people's emergencies. Evaluate every event rationally and see whether there really does have to be a meeting tomorrow at 7 am or tonight at 8 pm. Ask

whether the client really does need the report by tomorrow or whether they'll be okay if they get it the next day. There are nutters out there and they have no concept of reason or life away from work. Don't get caught up in their psycho-spiral.

- As a general rule, don't do business lunches. If you want to have a social lunch, go for it, but if the purpose is a business discussion then organise a cup of coffee or tea. This is a far more efficient use of your time.
- Learn to say no. This will be easier for some than others, but even if you are in the lower echelons of an organisation, understand that people will load you up with work until you fall over. You need to learn how to say 'enough' in a profes-sional way that respects the relationship with your boss and yet ensures your work life is sus-tainable.

Repairing relationships

- It's never too late to say sorry. Think about rela-tionships that are important to you, and if they are in poor shape, repair them.
- Spend some time and you will see that even the most fractured relationship can turn around into a warm, loving bond between two people. It will take time; your initial steps in repairing the rela-tionship may falter, but persevere.
- It is okay to tell someone that you love them and care for them, even though you may feel that they 'should know' this.

Preparing for the future while living for today

Make a five-year plan that identifies your goals for;

- Health and well-being
- Work and career
- Finances
- Relationships:
  - With your partner
  - With your friends
  - With your family
- Hobbies and interests
- Community activities.

Use a table like this:

Goals	Year 1	Year 2	Year 3	Year 4	Year 5
Health and wellbeing					
Work and career					
Finances					
Relationships: • Partner • Friends • Family					
Hobbies and interests					
Community activities					

- Your goals should build, year on year. Therefore if you want to get to a goal by year 5 then what does that mean you need to do by year 4, year 3, etc. This process will present you with a clear objective for what you need to do in year 1 (ie *now*) to achieve your year 5 goals.

- Break down each goal for year 1 into a set of activities required to achieve the goal. For example, if you have a goal to develop a lower golf handicap, the activities would include a weekly golf game and some weekly practice or coaching. If the goal was to repair a fractured relationship with someone you love, the activity list might include allocating time each week to spend with the person and perhaps a monthly special event to go to with the person.
- Your goals should include input from those that you love so that they will be supportive of your goals and also help you gain some perspective on the goals.
- Friday afternoon review: Look at your goals at the end of every week and honestly ask yourself if you have made progress towards each goal and if you have undertaken the activities that you said you would. Do *not* just focus on your work achievements, but rather look at every area with the same focus and effort. If you have slipped up, then make some changes in your diary for the coming week and recalibrate your activity set.

Taking the final step

Grant yourself half an hour to really think about your life. Sit quietly somewhere where you can be alone, without noise or interruption. Close your eyes and think about how you want your life to be eulogised. What do you want people to say about you when you are gone? What do you want to leave behind in terms of the value you have added to the lives of others?

What really matters to you? Do you feel you are living a life that you are truly proud of, and do you feel you are doing justice to the people that care for you and need you? Do you feel your life is sustainable or are you just surviving, just coping?

Capture these thoughts and capture the vision of the life you want to live. Commit to making changes that will ensure you are on a path to a future that you have designed. Disregard how you might be seen by your work peers and take solace in the fact that you are taking control of your life.

Work out what matters to you and then align your effort and focus accordingly. Do this and you will have the best chance of a successful life—a sustainable, happy, successful life.

FURTHER READING

Fernando Bartolome & Paul Lee Evans, 'Must success cost so much?', *Harvard Business Review*, March–April 1980.

Charles Birch & David Paul, *Life and Work,* UNSW Press, Sydney, 2003.

David Boyle, *The Sum of Our Discontent*, Texere, New York, 2001.

Jim Collins, *Good to Great*, Random House, New York, 2001.

Robert Cooper & Ayman Sawaf, *Executive EQ*, Orion Publishing Group, London, 1997.

Stephen Covey, *First Things First*, Simon & Schuster, New York, 1996.

Steven Covey, *Principle Centred Leadership*, Simon & Schuster, New York, 1992.

Stephen Covey, *The Seven Habits of Highly Effective People*, Melbourne: The Business Library, 1990.

David Dotlich & Peter Cairo, *Why CEOs Fail*, Jossey-Bass, New York, 2003.

Richard Eckersley, *Well & Good*, Text Publishing, Melbourne, 2004.

Sydney Finkelstein, *Why Smart Executives Fail*, Portfolio, New York, 2003.

Daniel Goleman, *Emotional Intelligence*, Bloomsbury Publishing, London, 1996.

Daniel Goleman, *Primal Leadership*, Harvard Business School Press, New York, 2004.

Daniel Goleman, *Working with Emotional Intelligence,* Bloomsbury Publishing, London, 1998.

Charles Handy, *The Empty Raincoat*, Hutchison, London, 1994.

Charles Handy, *The Hungry Spirit*, Hutchinson, London, 1997.

Arlie Hochschild, *Second Shift*, Penguin, New York, 1989.

Arlie Hochschild, *The Commercialisation of Intimate Life*, University of California Press, California, 2003.

Arlie Hochschild, *The Time Bind*, Owl Books, New York, 2001.

John Holder, *The Tao of Leadership,* Wildwood House Ltd, London, 1987.

William Joyce, Nitin Nohira & Bruce Roberson, *What Really Works*, Harper Business, New York, 2003.

John Kotter & James Heskett, *Corporate Culture and Performance*, Free Press, NY, 1992.

Patrick Lencioni, 'Make Your Values Mean Something', *Harvard Business Review*, July 2000.

Michael Leunig, *Poems 1972-2002*, Penguin, Australia, 2003.

David Maister, *Practice What You Preach*, Free Press, New York, 2002.

Abraham Maslow, *Maslow on Management*, Wiley and Sons, New York, 1998.

Karen Morley, *Mount Eliza Business School Leadership Index*, 2004

John O'Neill, *The Paradox of Success*, McGraw-Hill, London, 1993

Rob Parsons, *Heart of Success*, Hodder & Stoughton, London, 2002.

Sogyal Rinpoche, *The Tibetan Book of Living and Dying*, Rider, UK, 1994

Lucy West & Mike Milan, *The Reflecting Glass*, Palgrave McMillan, New York, 2001.

John Zenger & Joseph Folkman, *The Extraordinary Leader*, McGraw-Hill, New York, 2002.